Elly Ruth's Designs
for the
Adult Coloring Artist

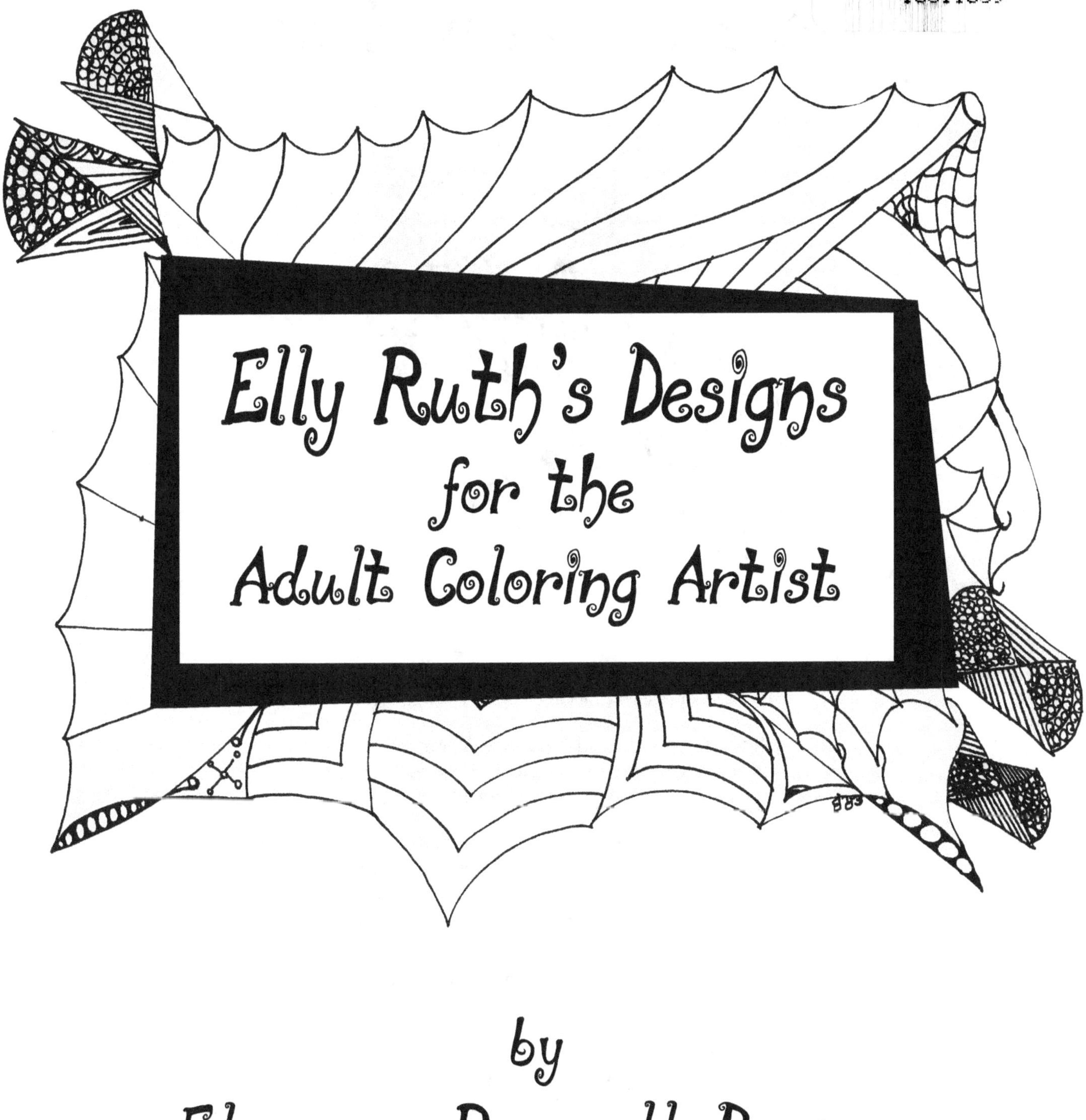

by

Eleanor Russell Brown

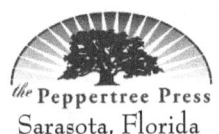
the Peppertree Press
Sarasota, Florida

Let Your Colors Soar

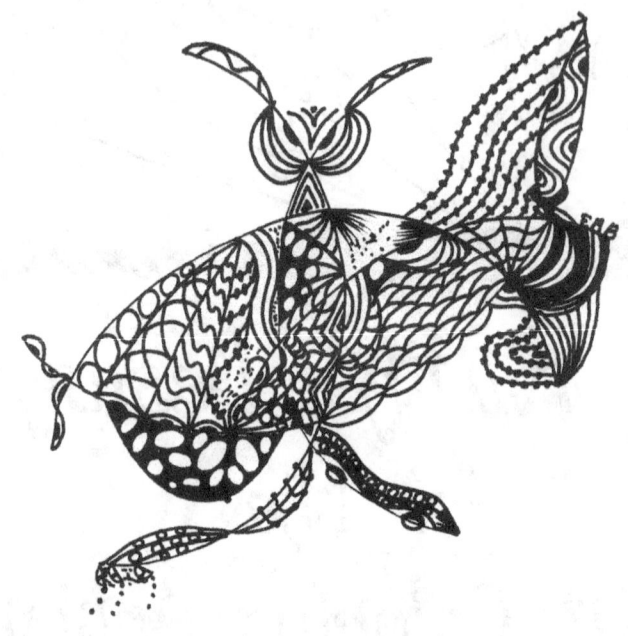

For information regarding permission,
call 941-922-2662 or contact us at our website:
www.peppertreepublishing.com or write to:
the Peppertree Press, LLC.
Attention: Publisher
1269 First Street, Suite 7
Sarasota, Florida 34236

ISBN: 978-1-61493-422-6

Library of Congress Number: 2016900910

Printed January 2016

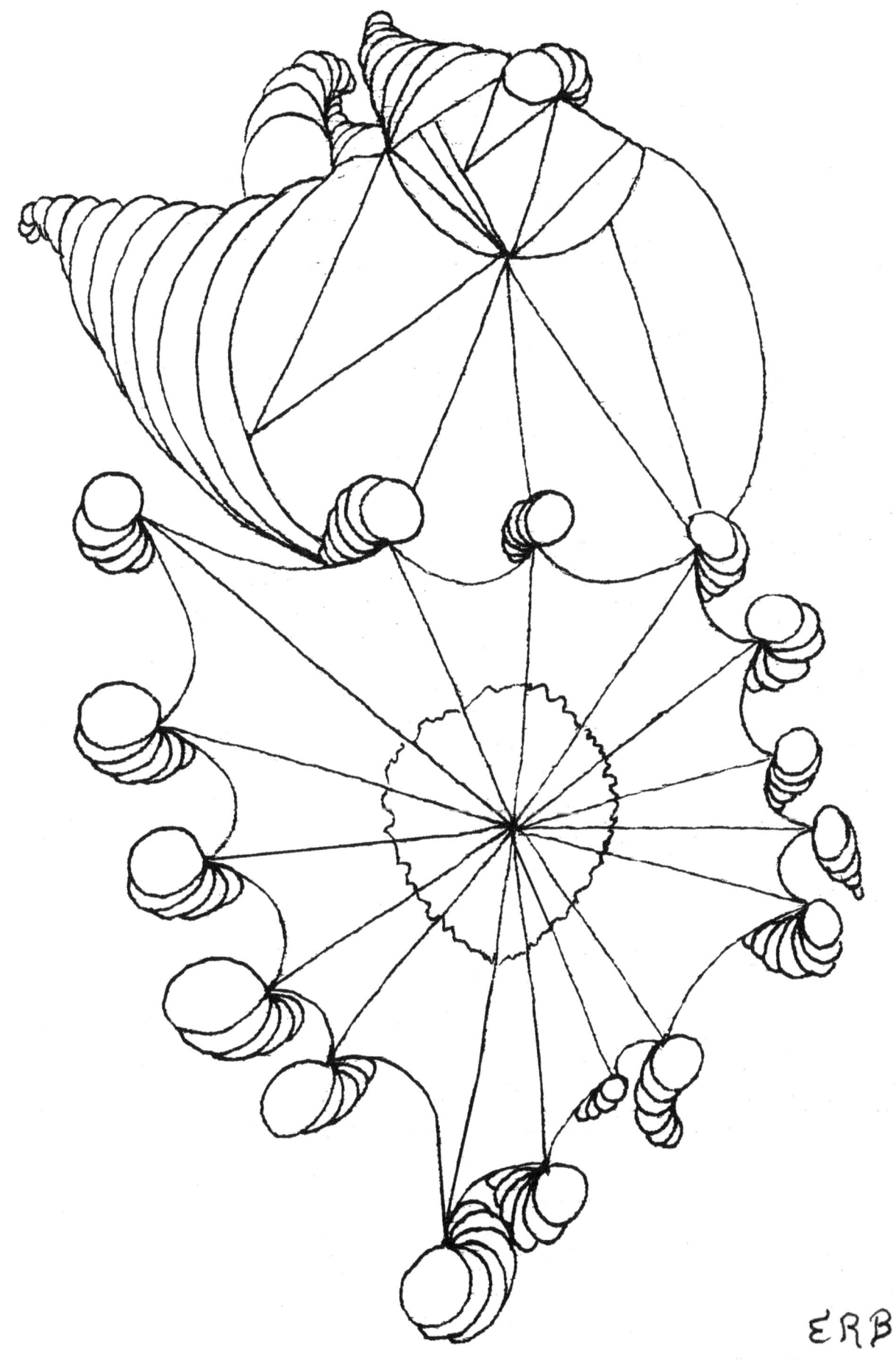

ERB

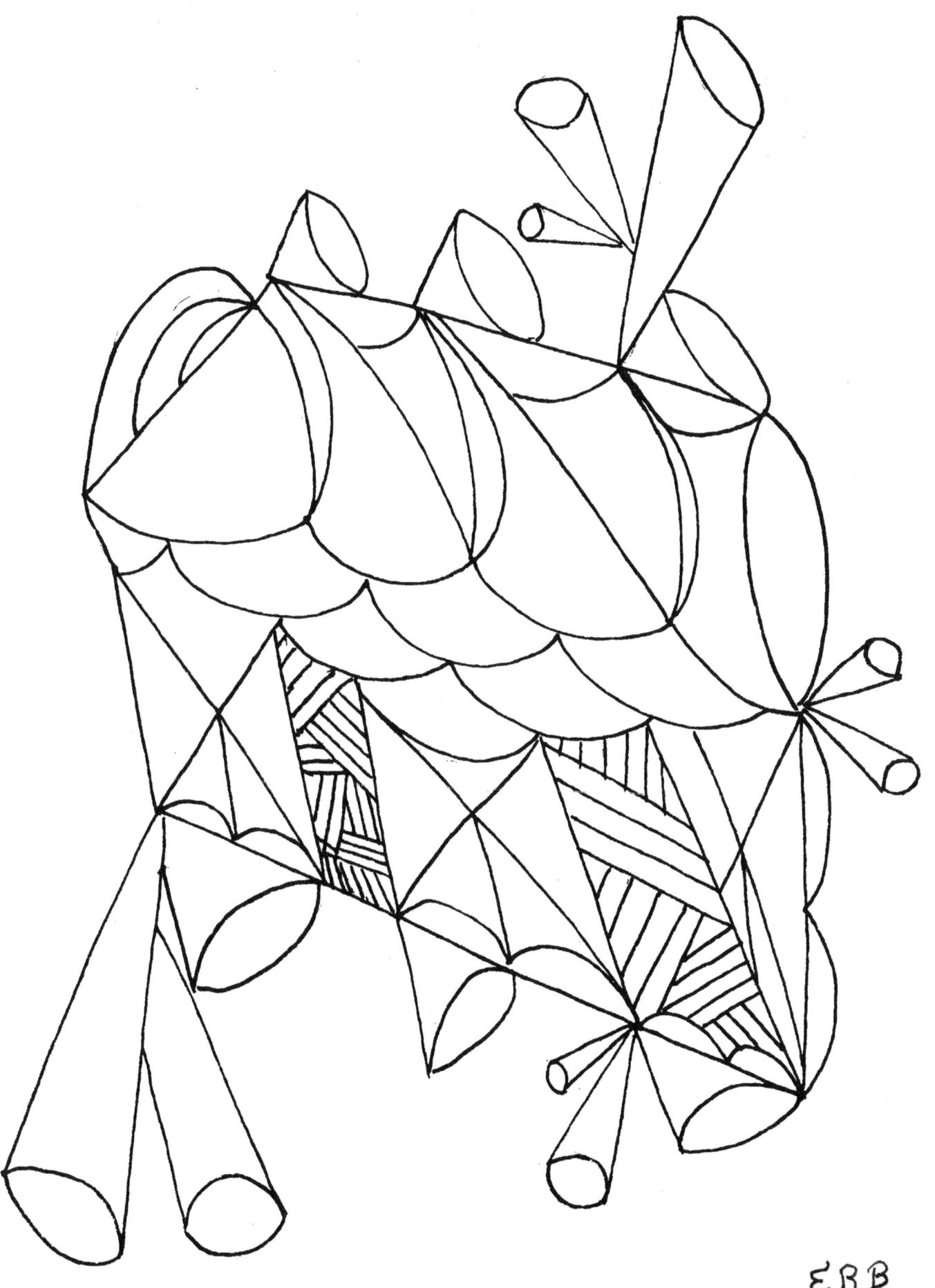

ERB

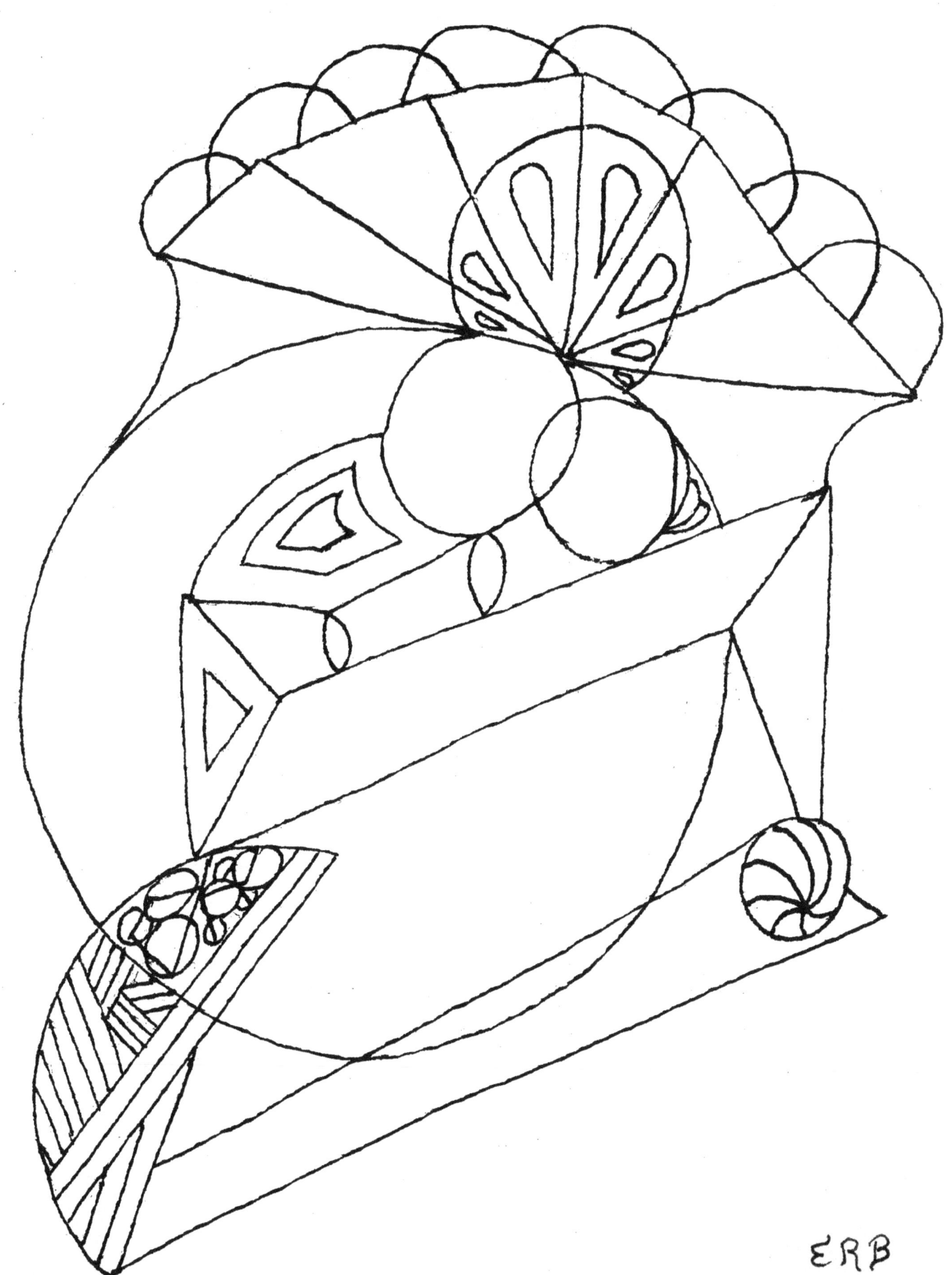

ERB

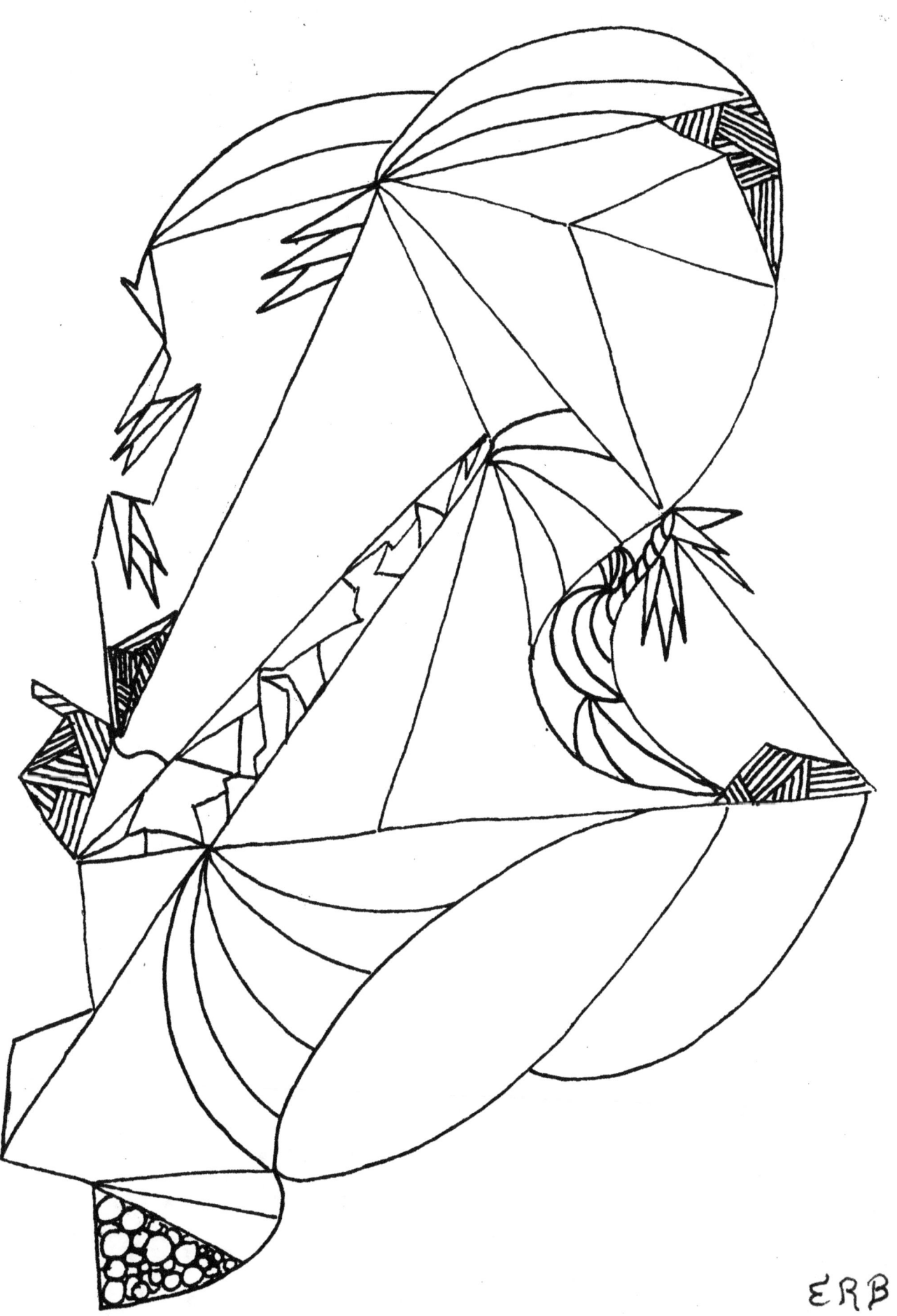

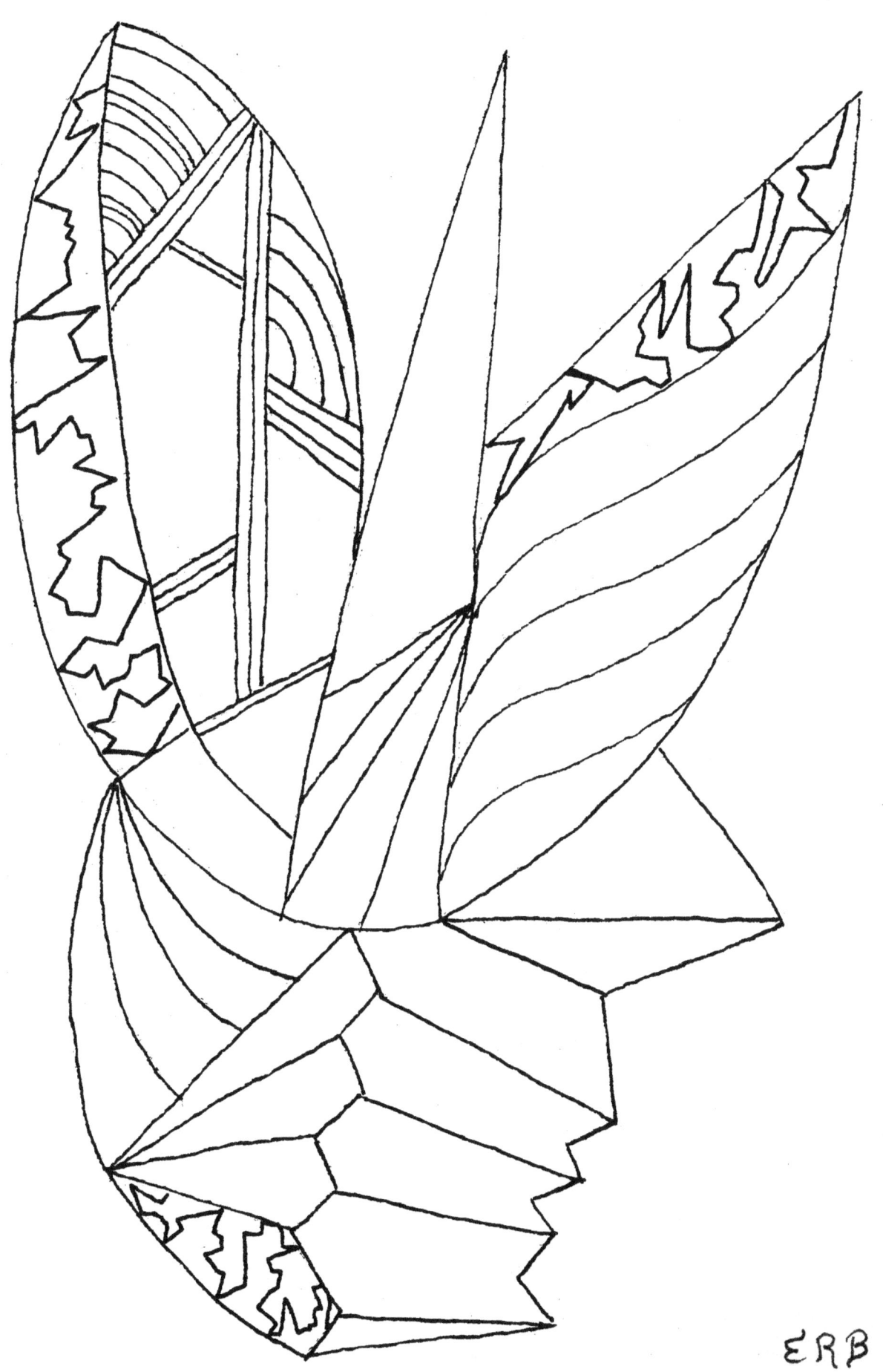

ERB

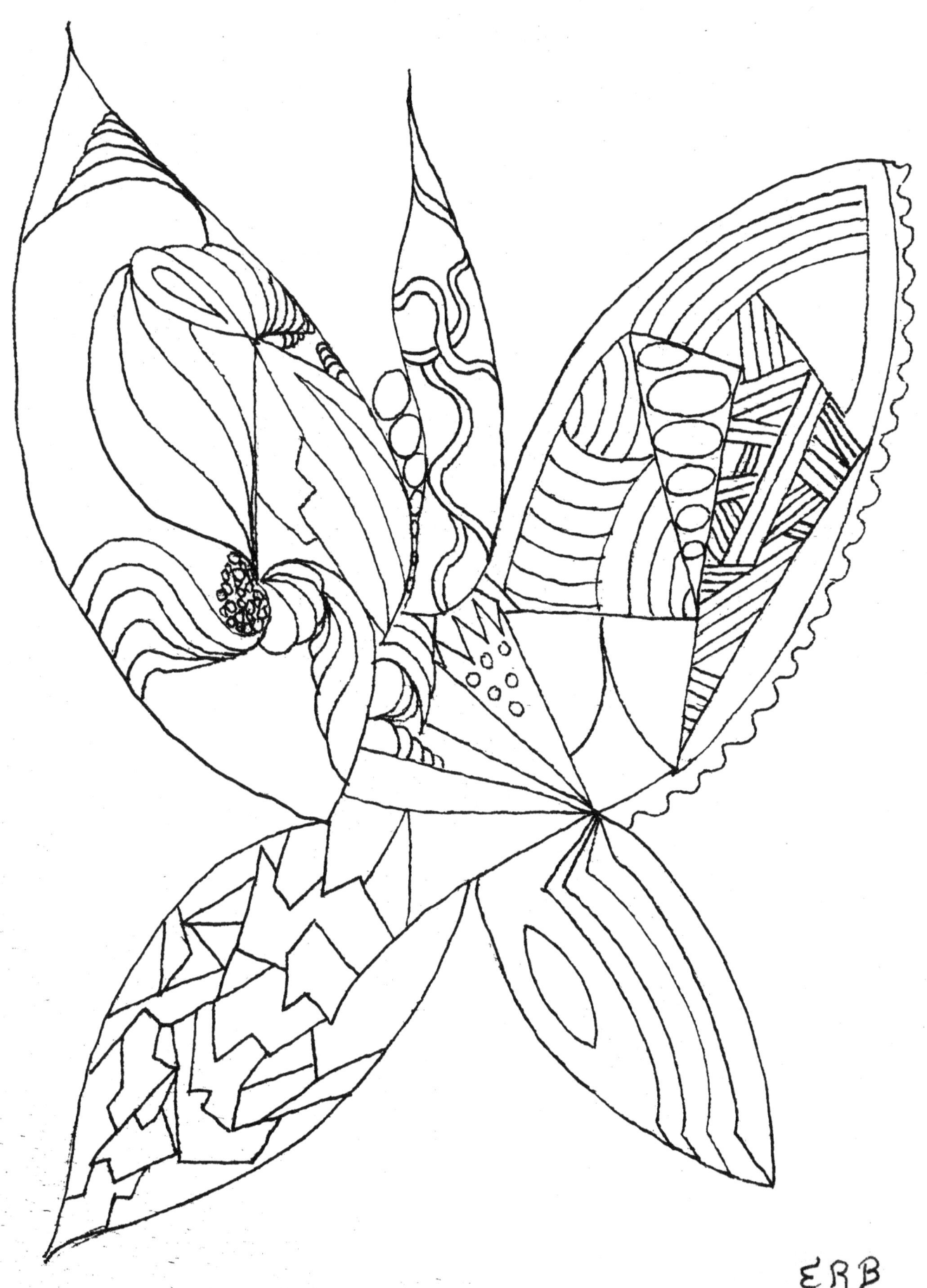

ERB

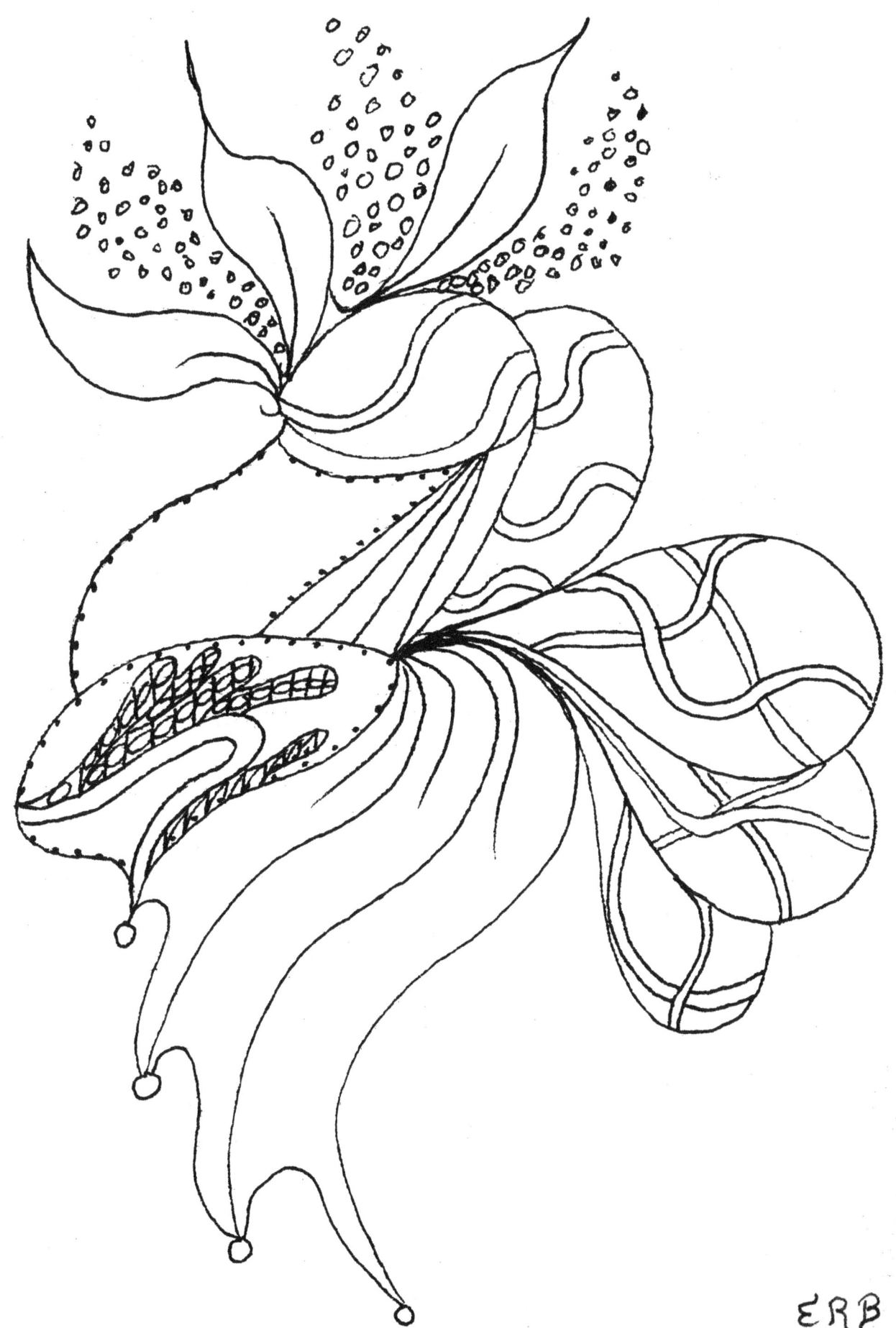

ERB

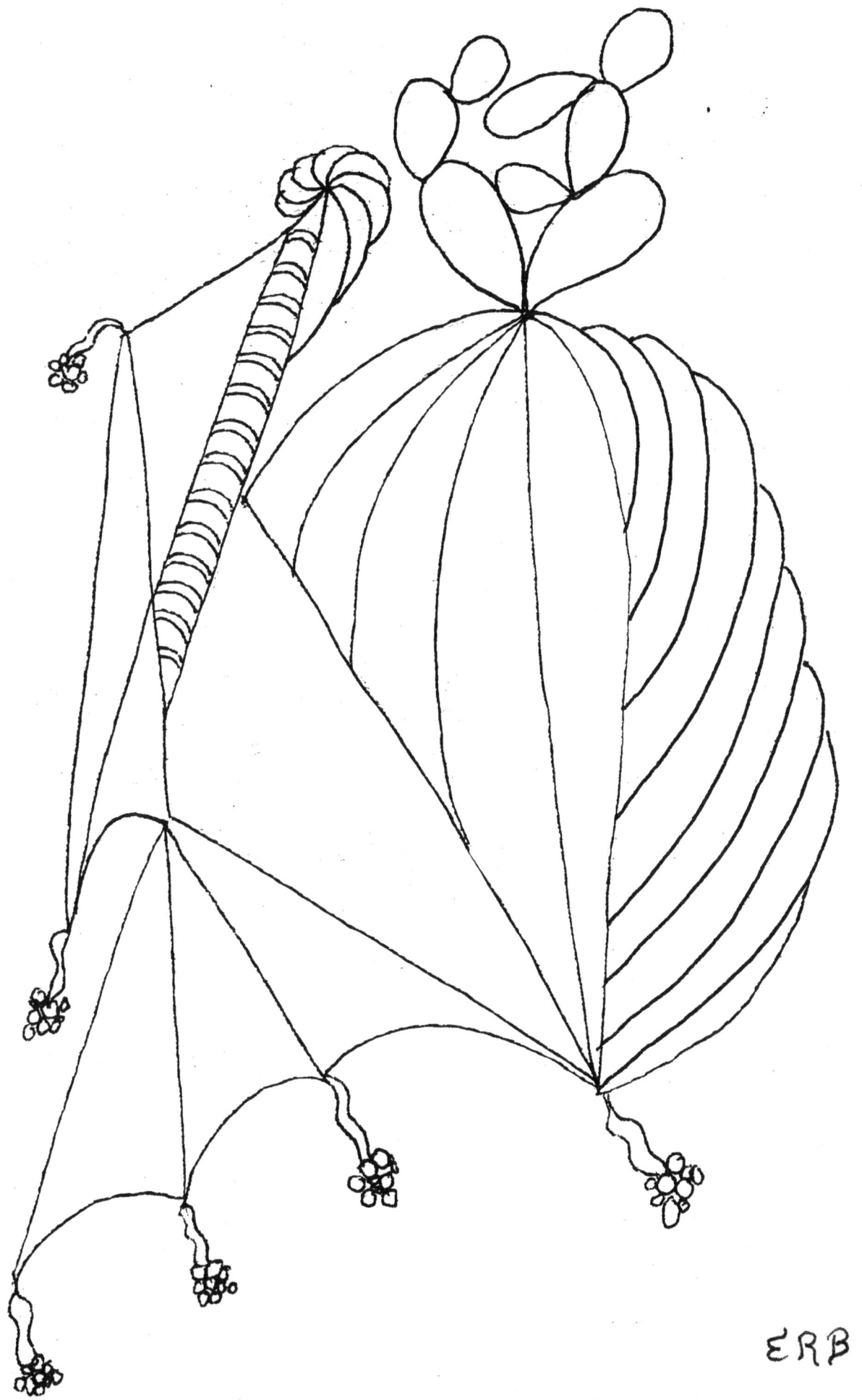

ERB

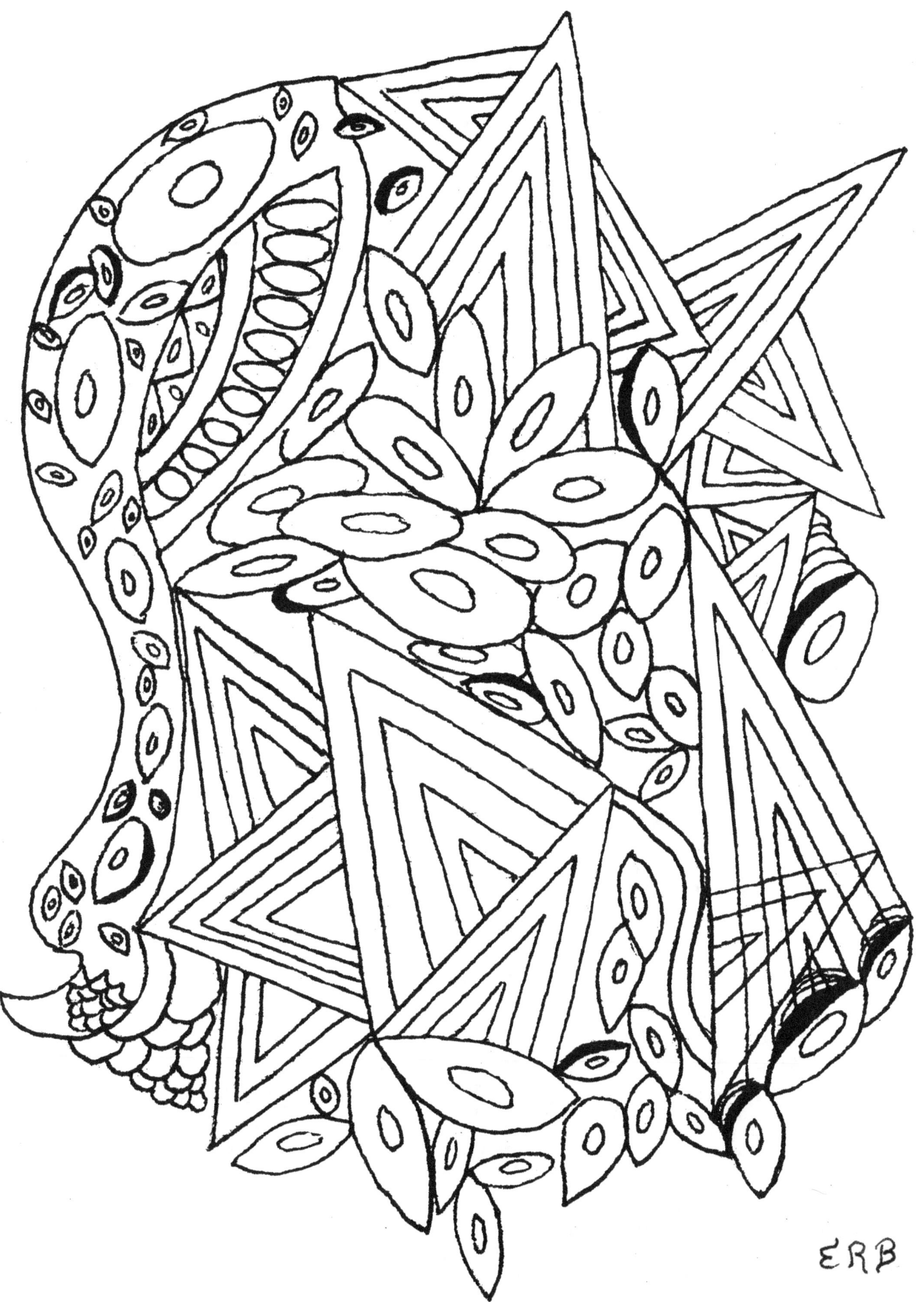

ERB

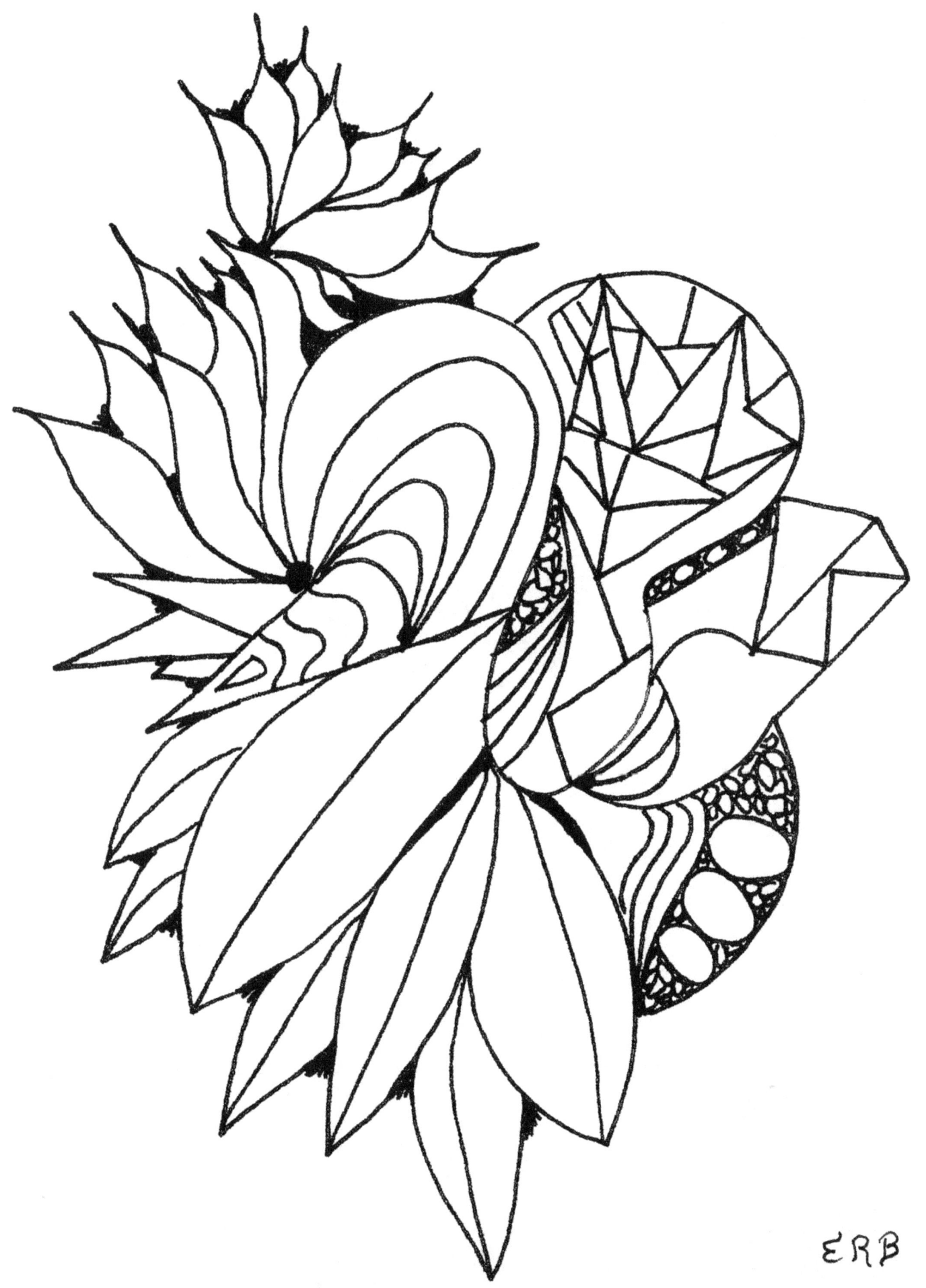

ERB

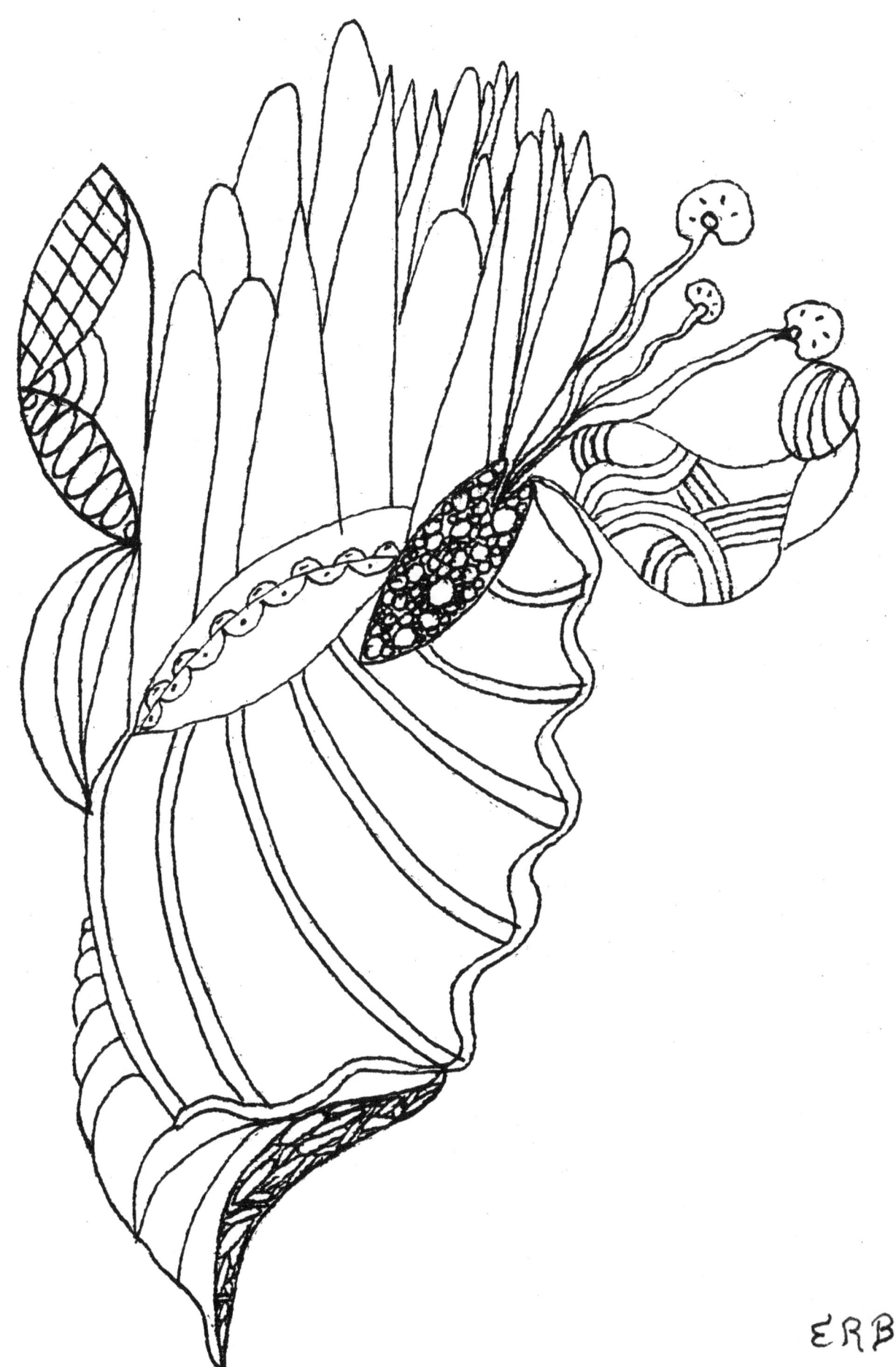

ERB

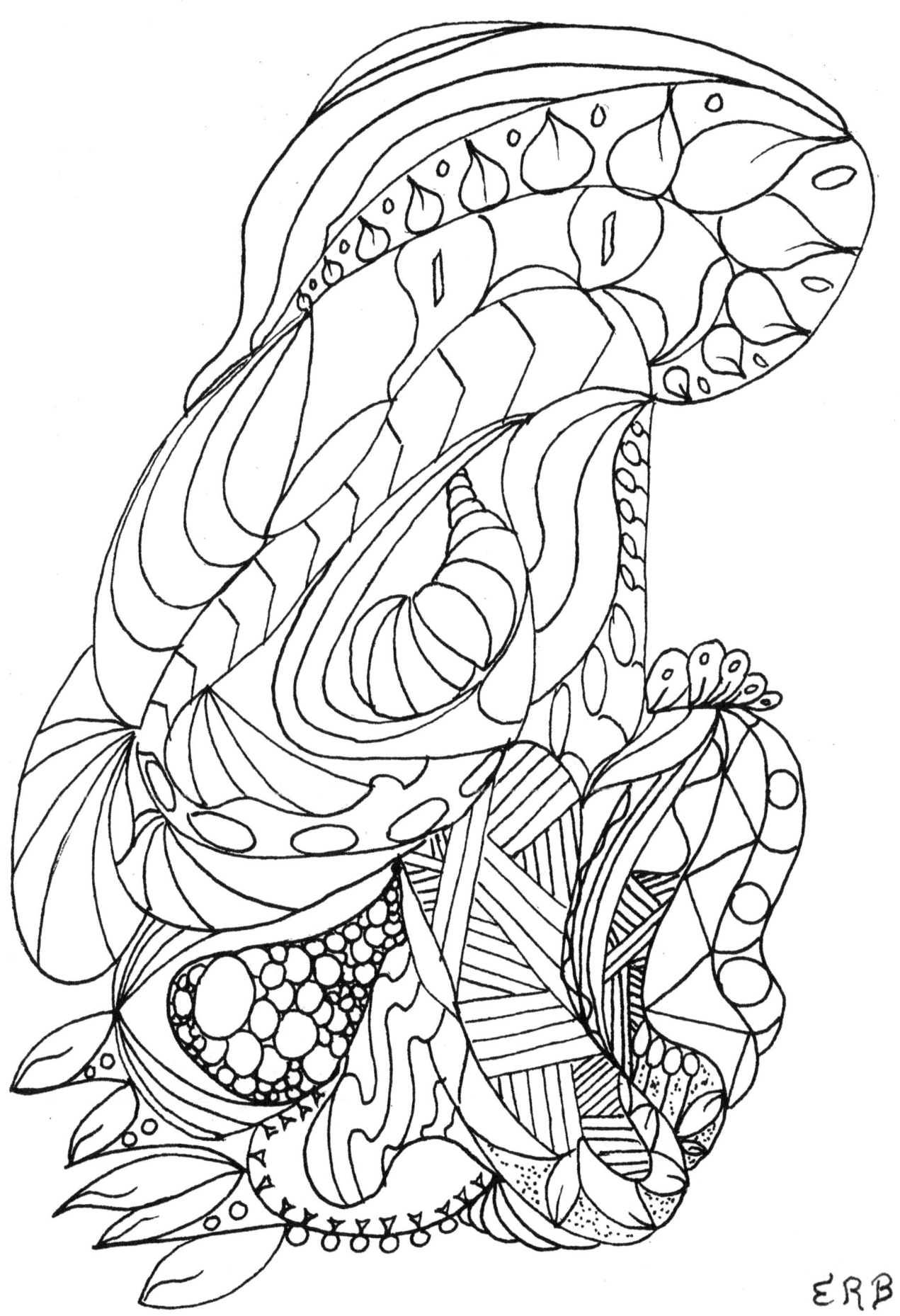

ERB

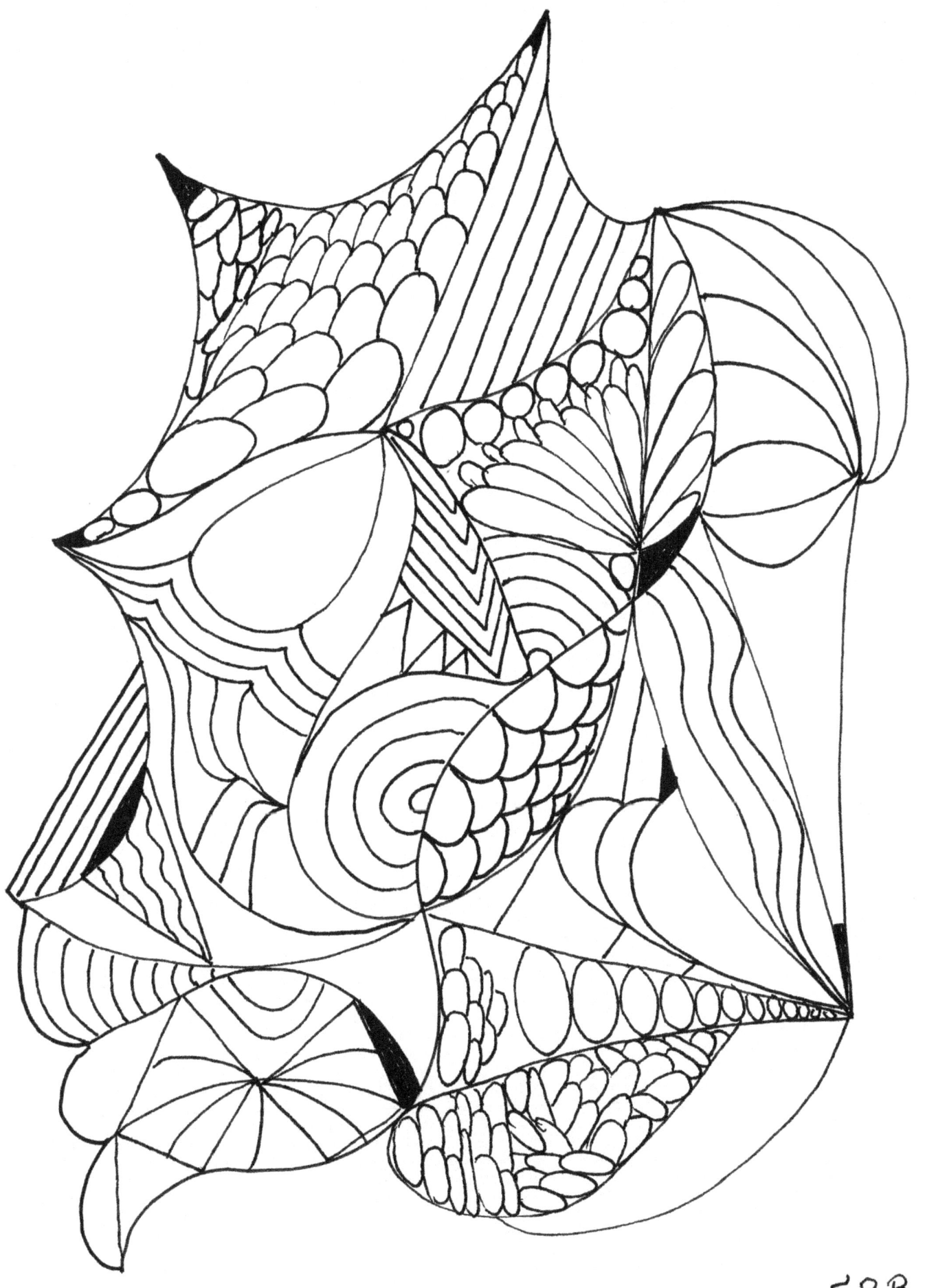

ERB

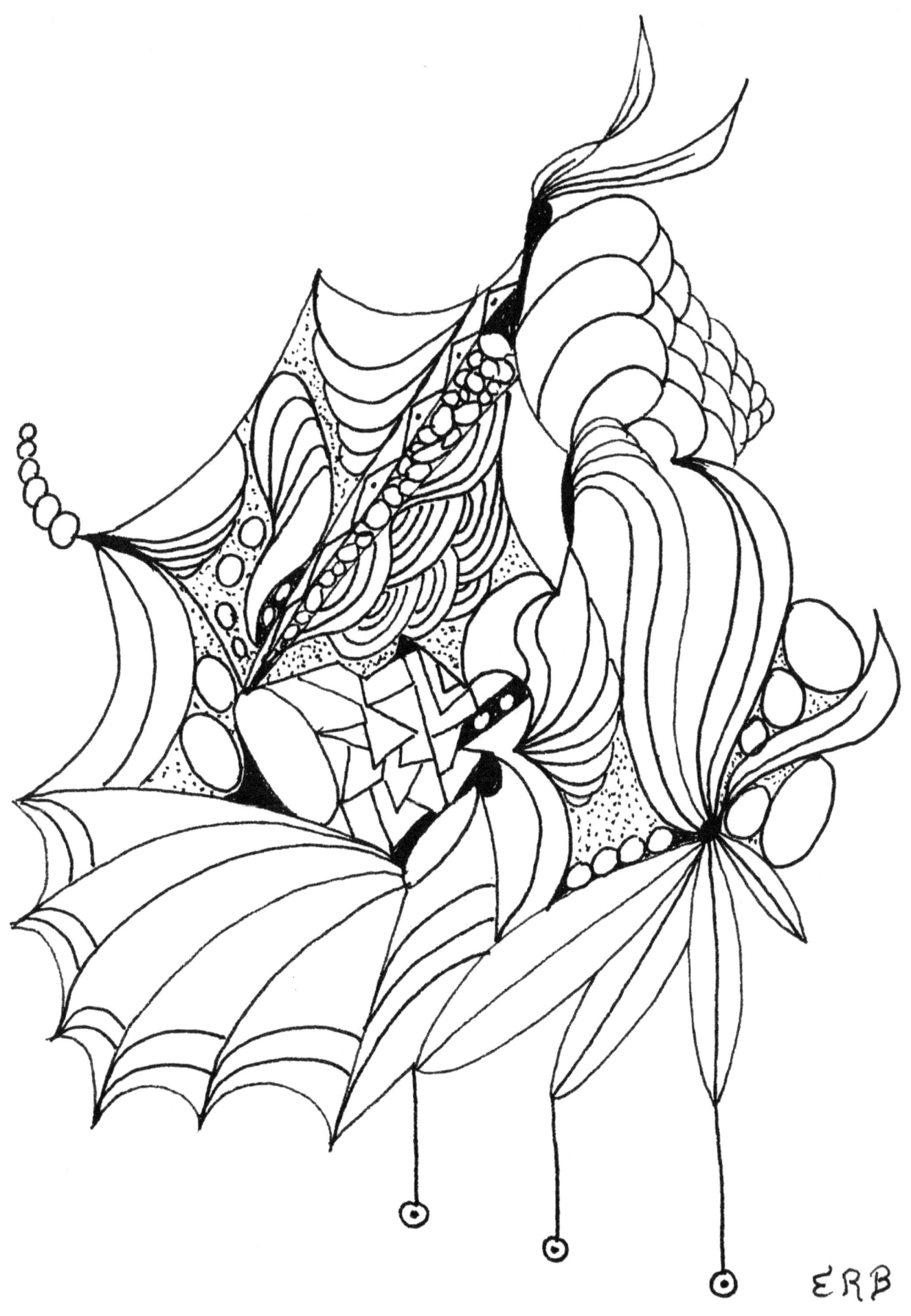

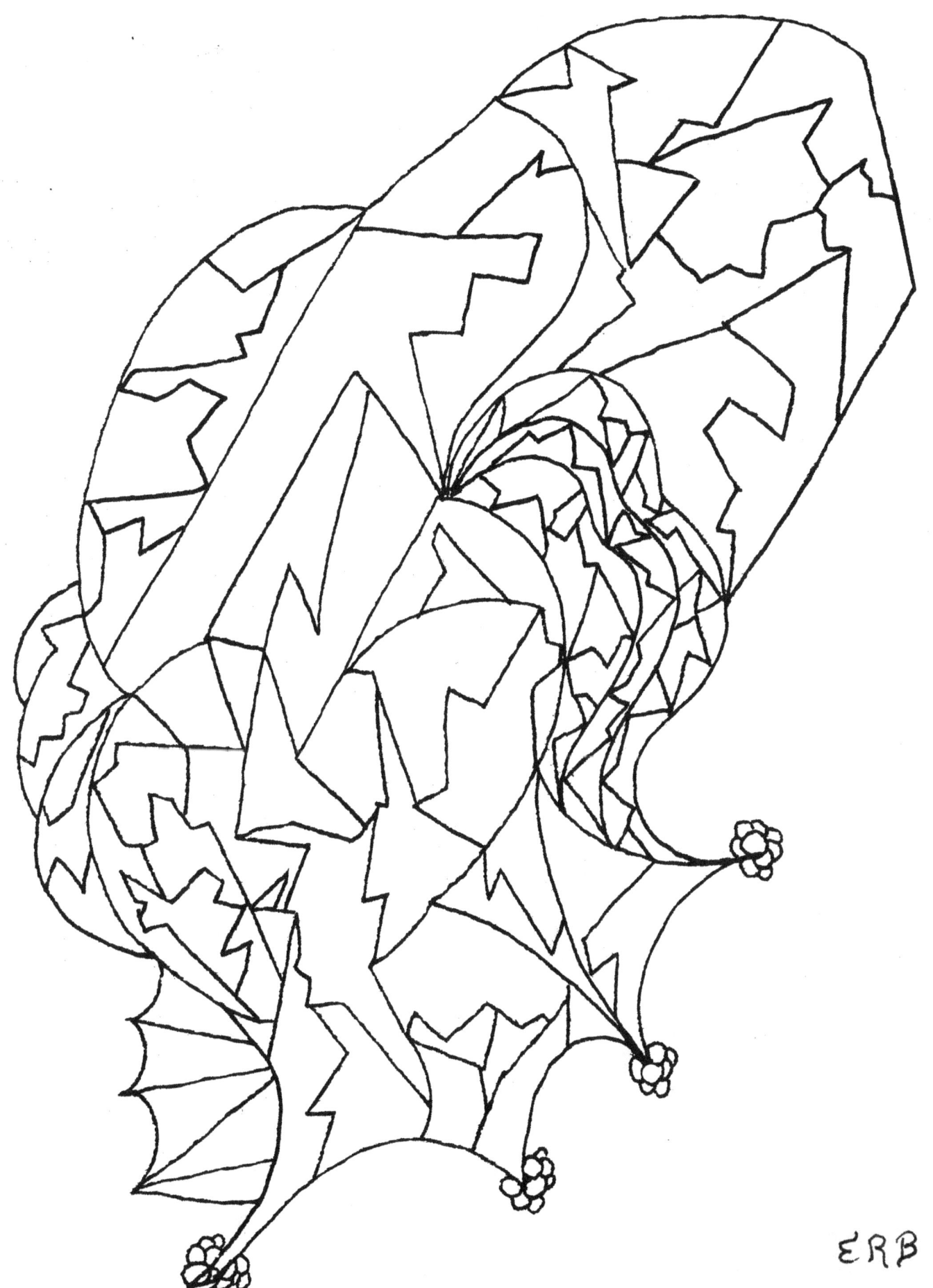

ERB

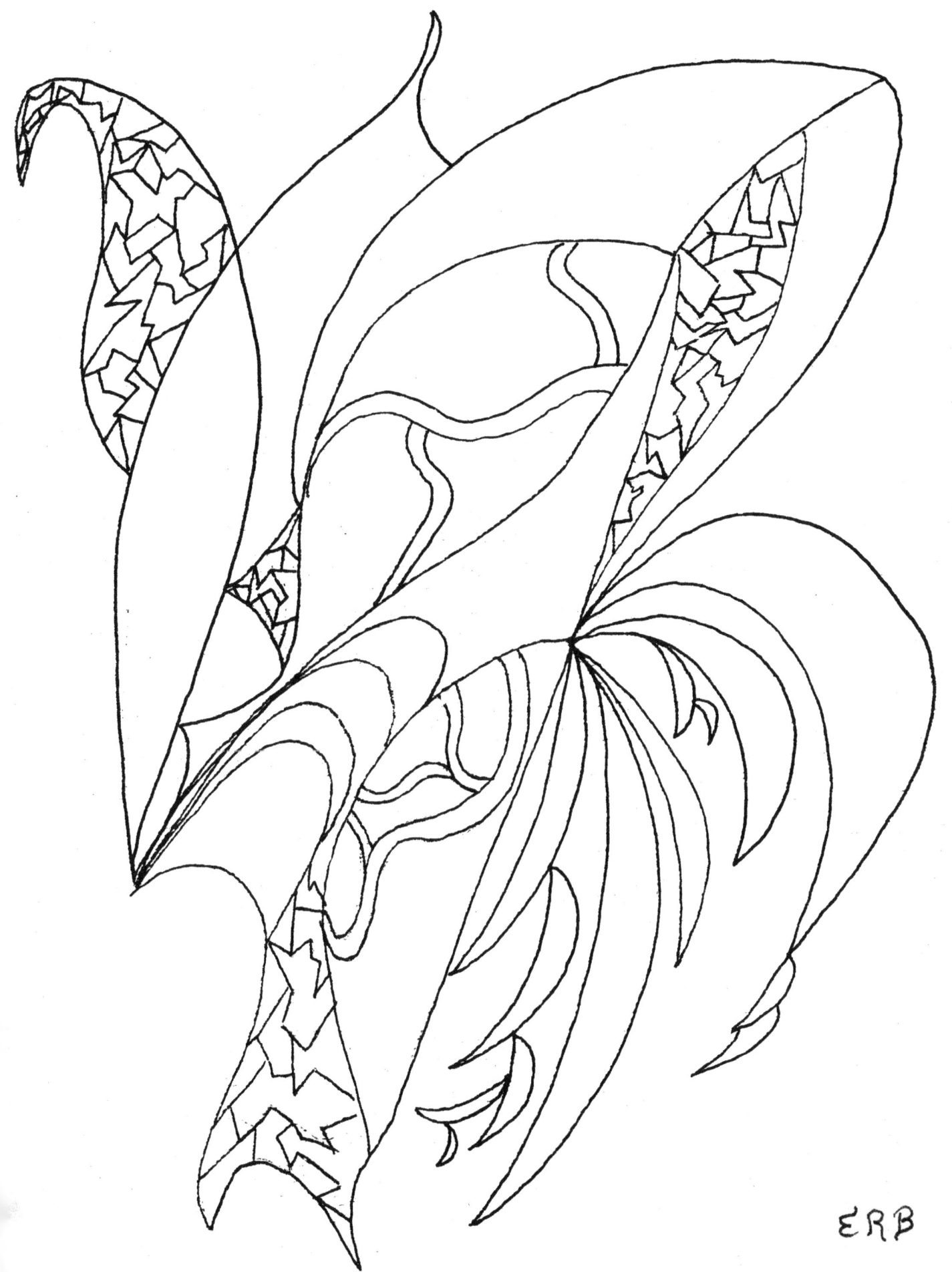

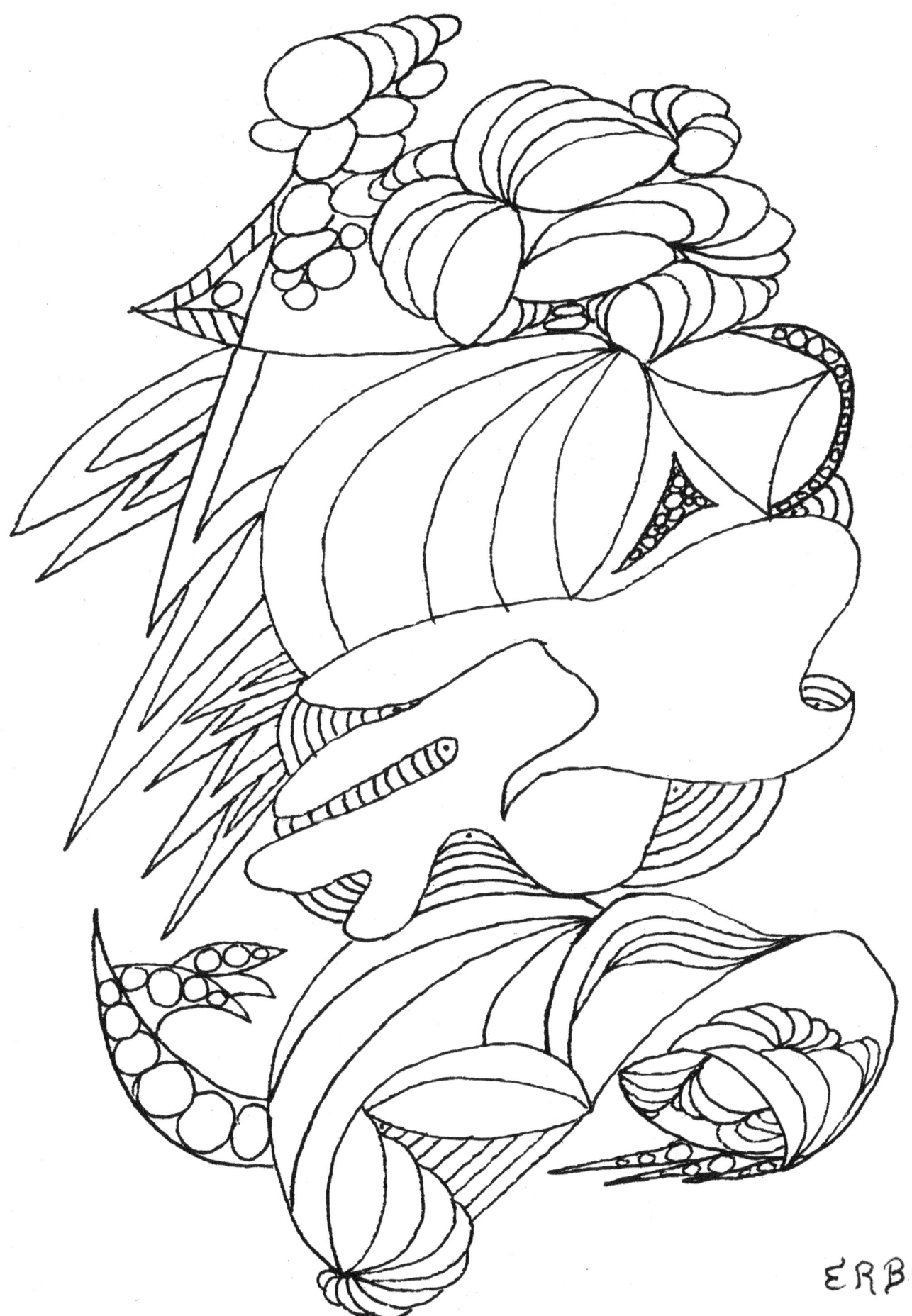

ERB

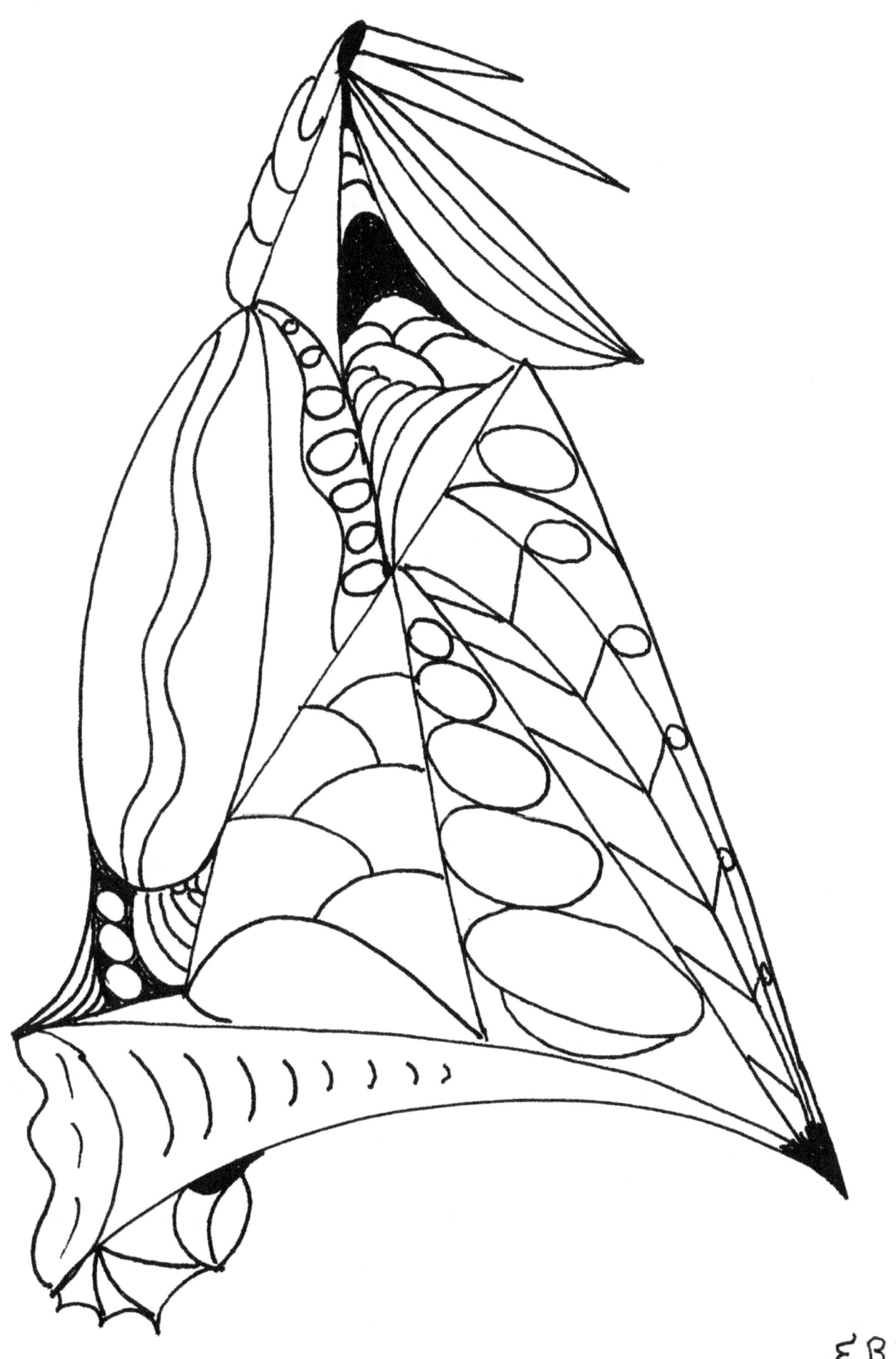

ERB

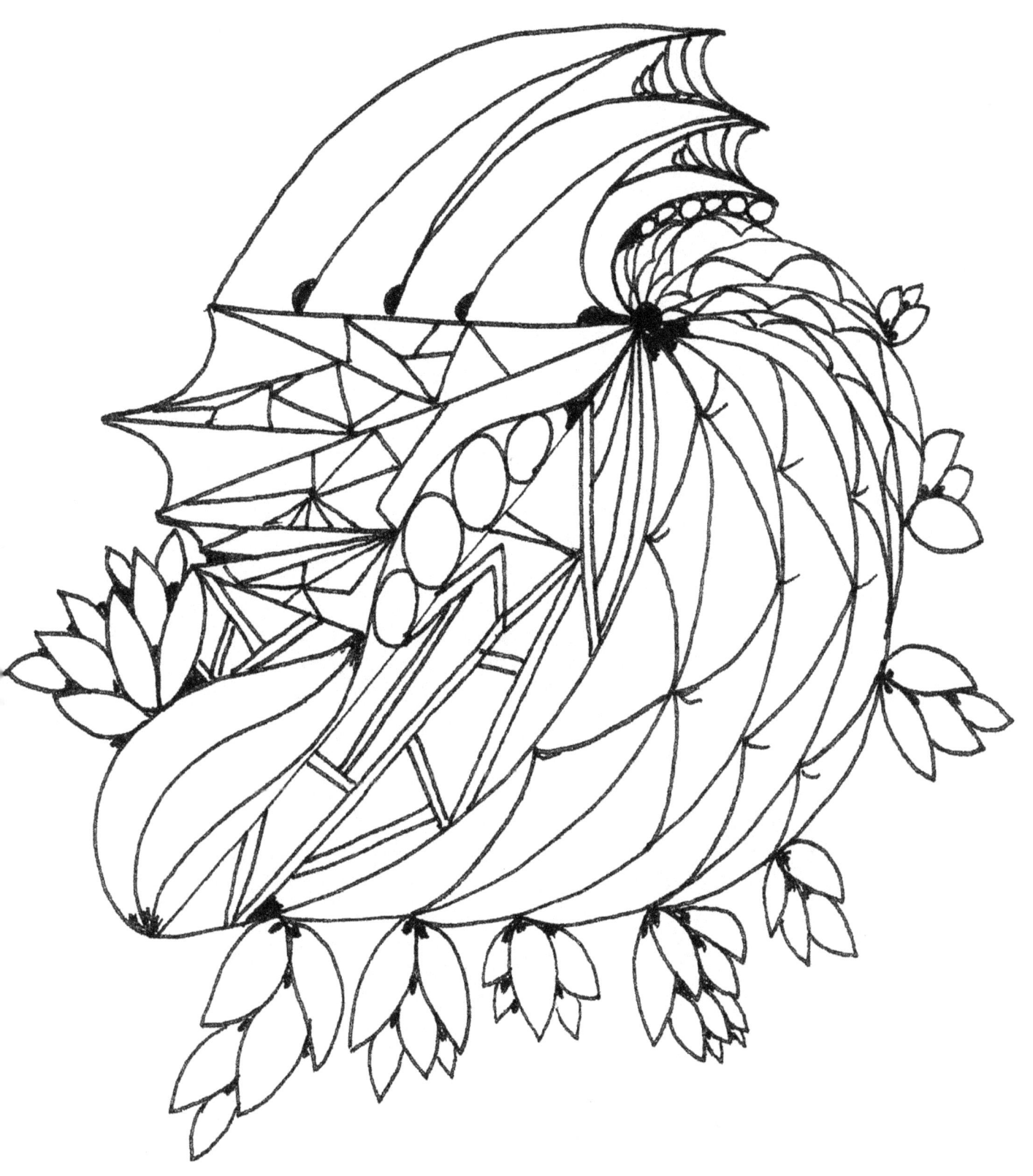

ERB

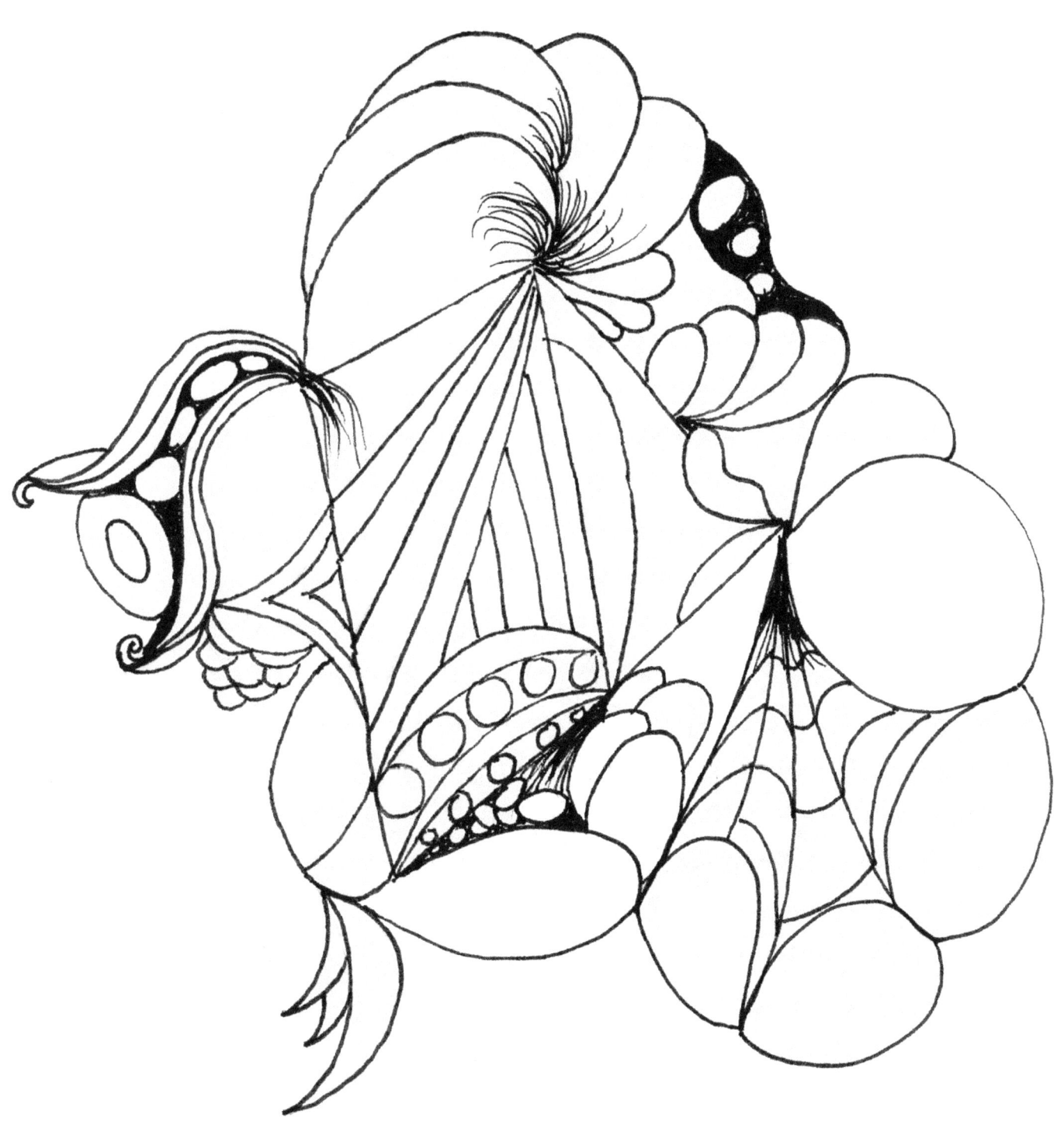

ERB

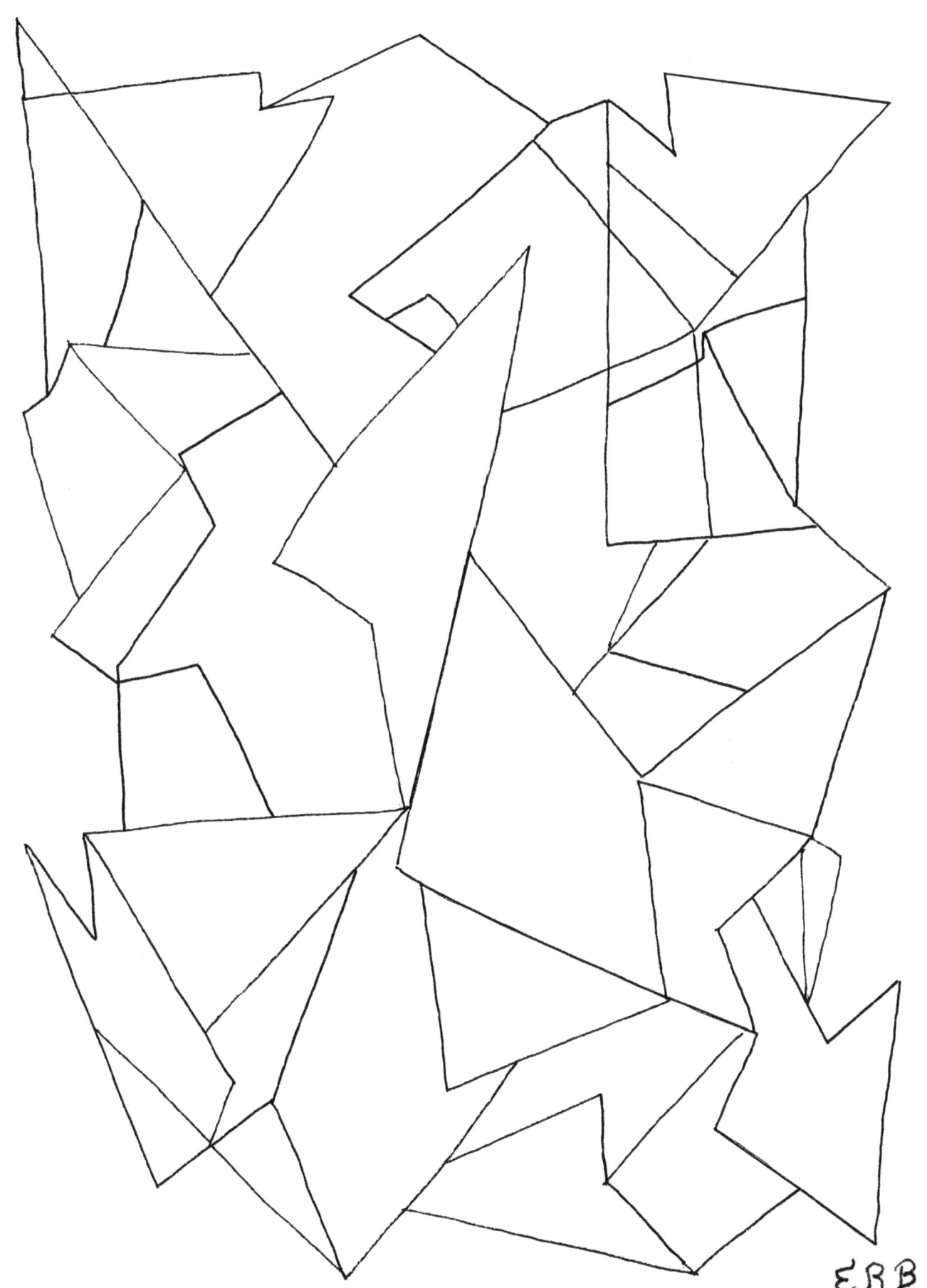

ERB

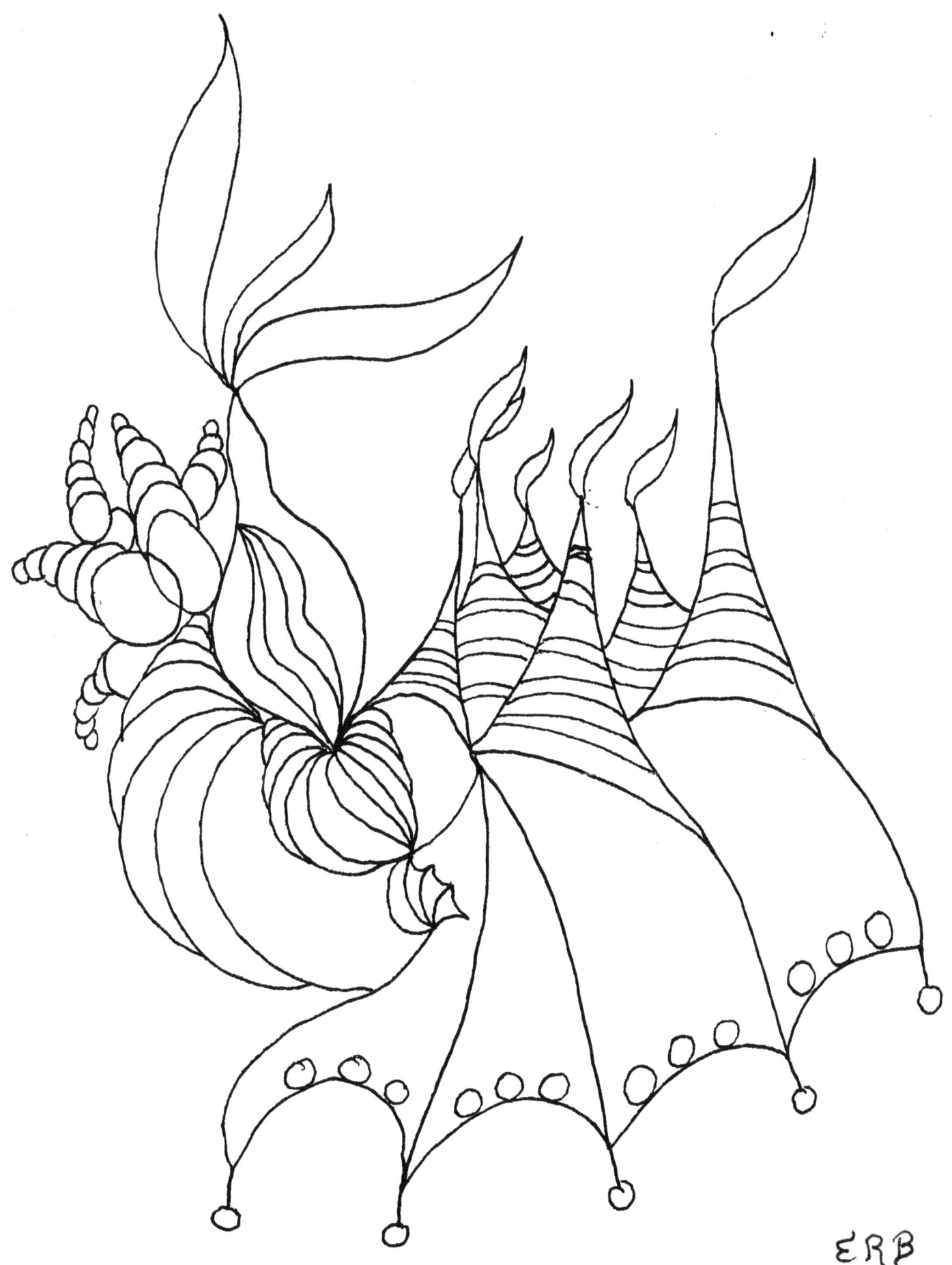

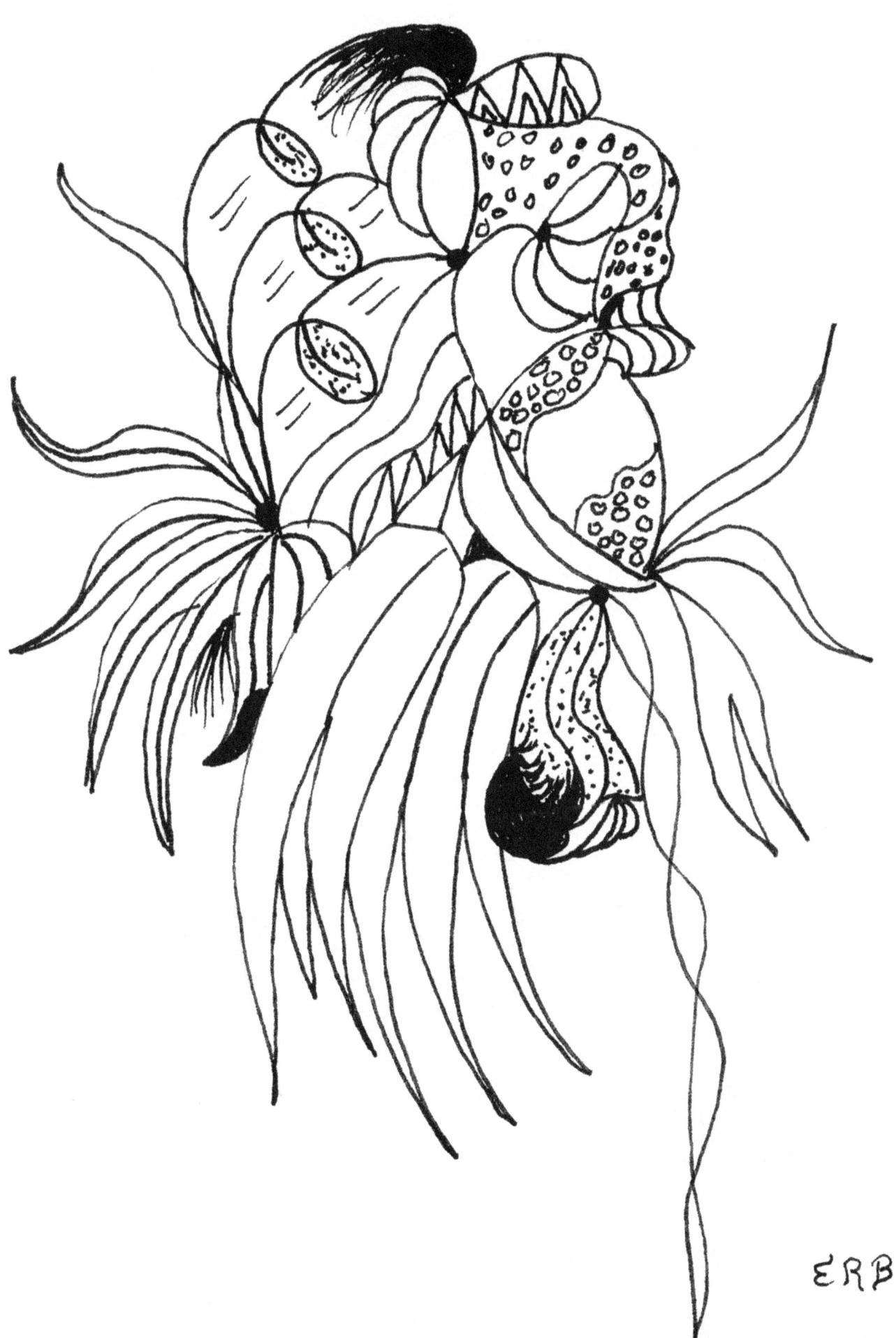

ERB

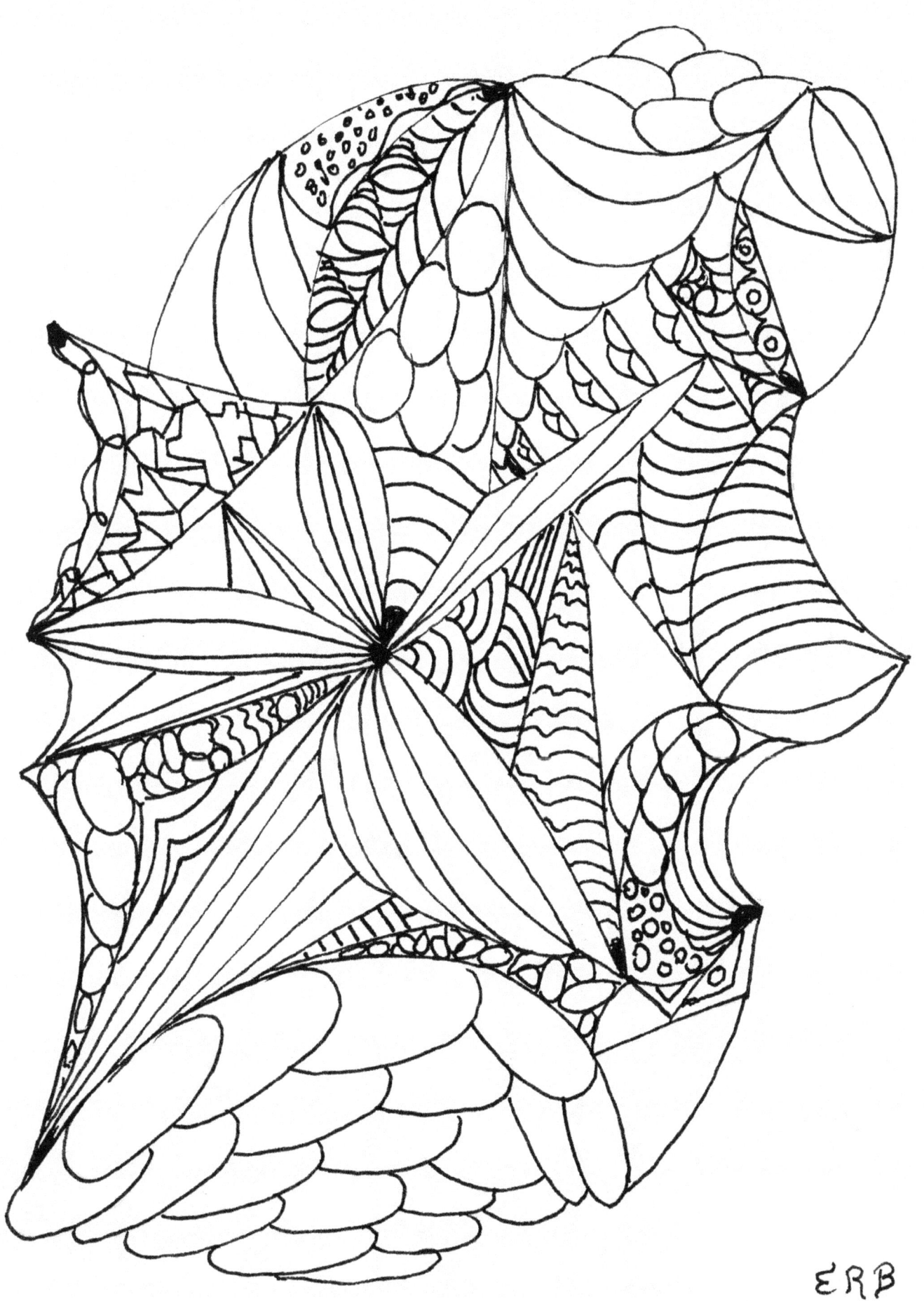

ERB

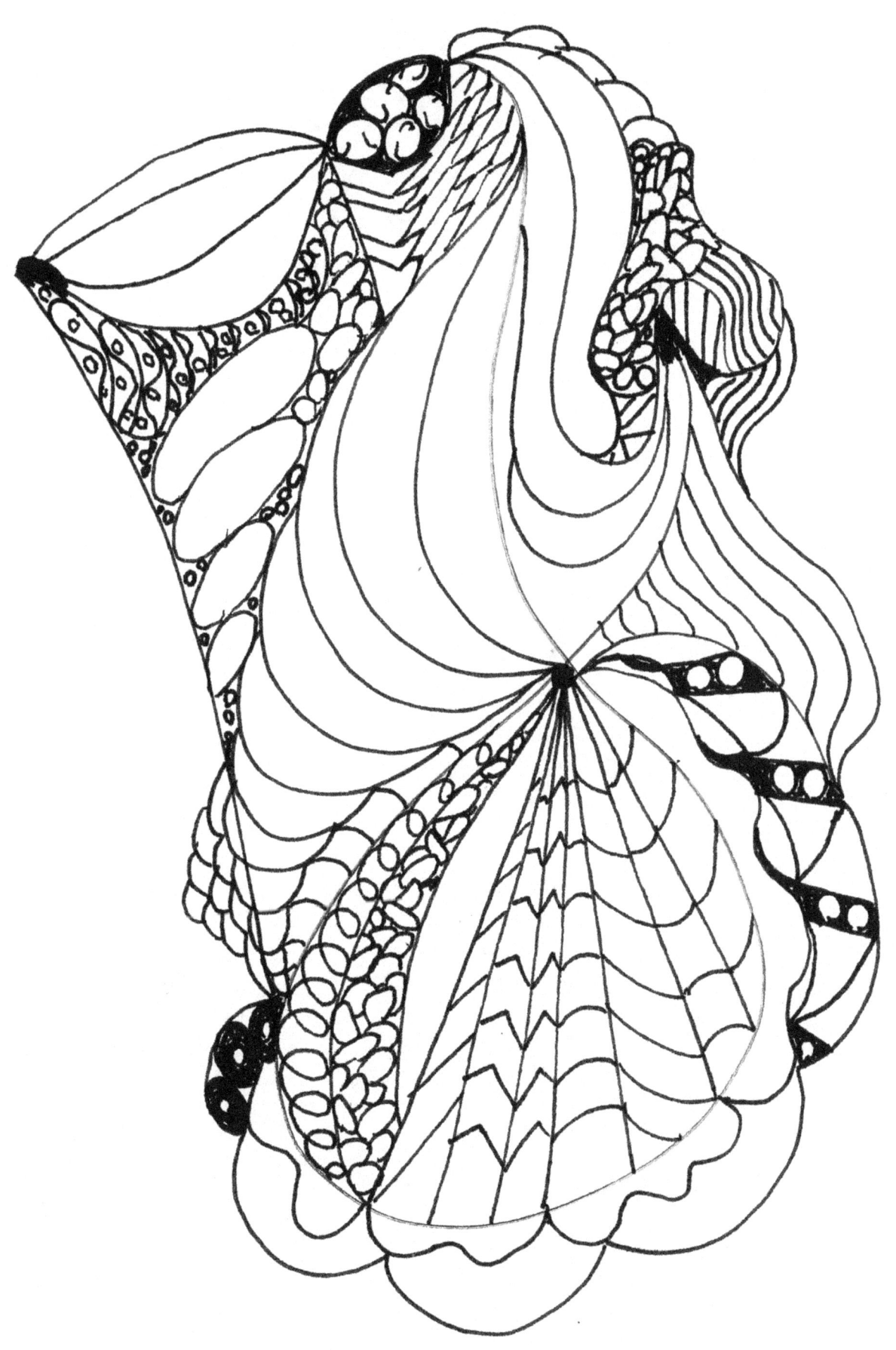

ERB

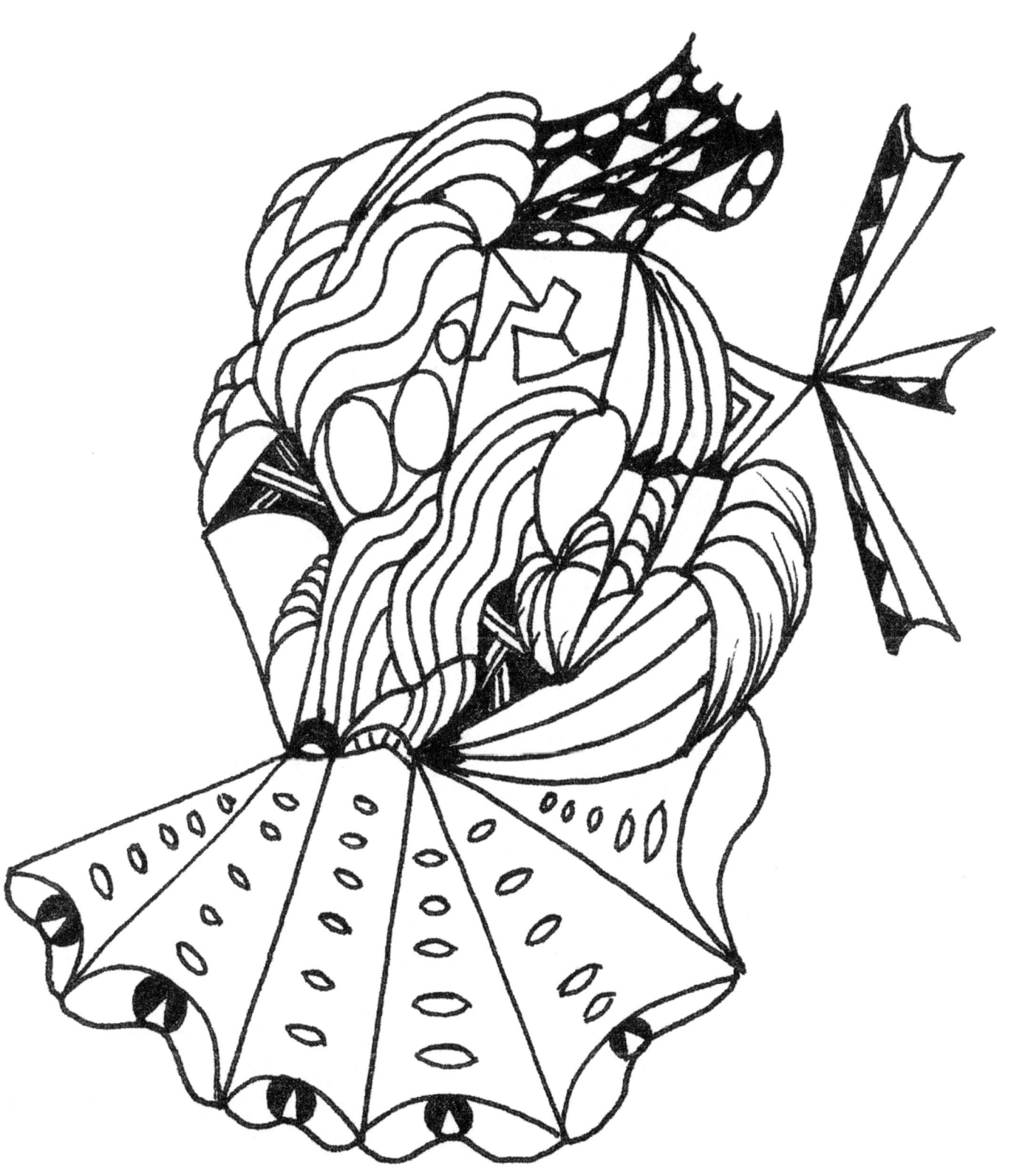

ERB

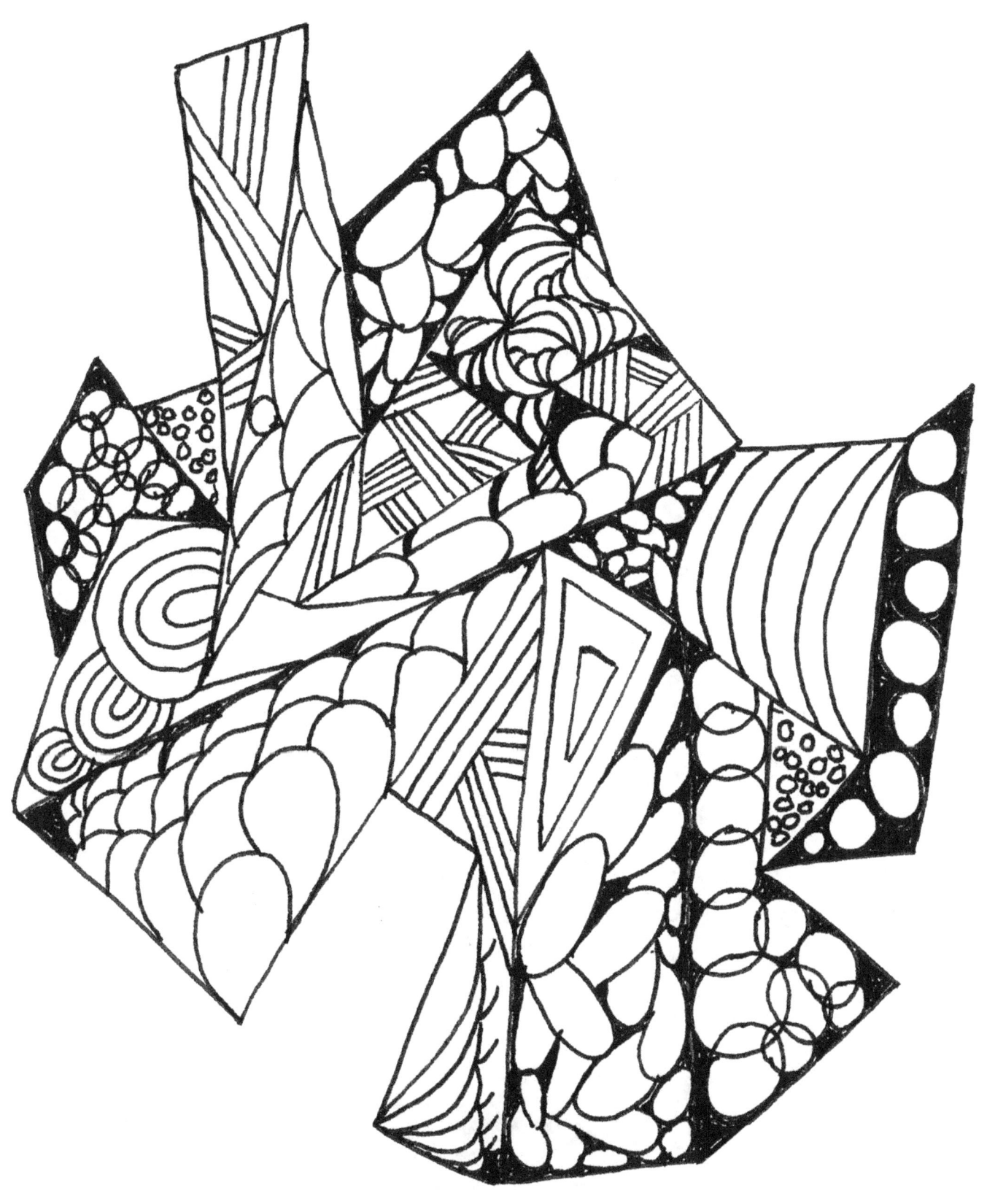

ERB

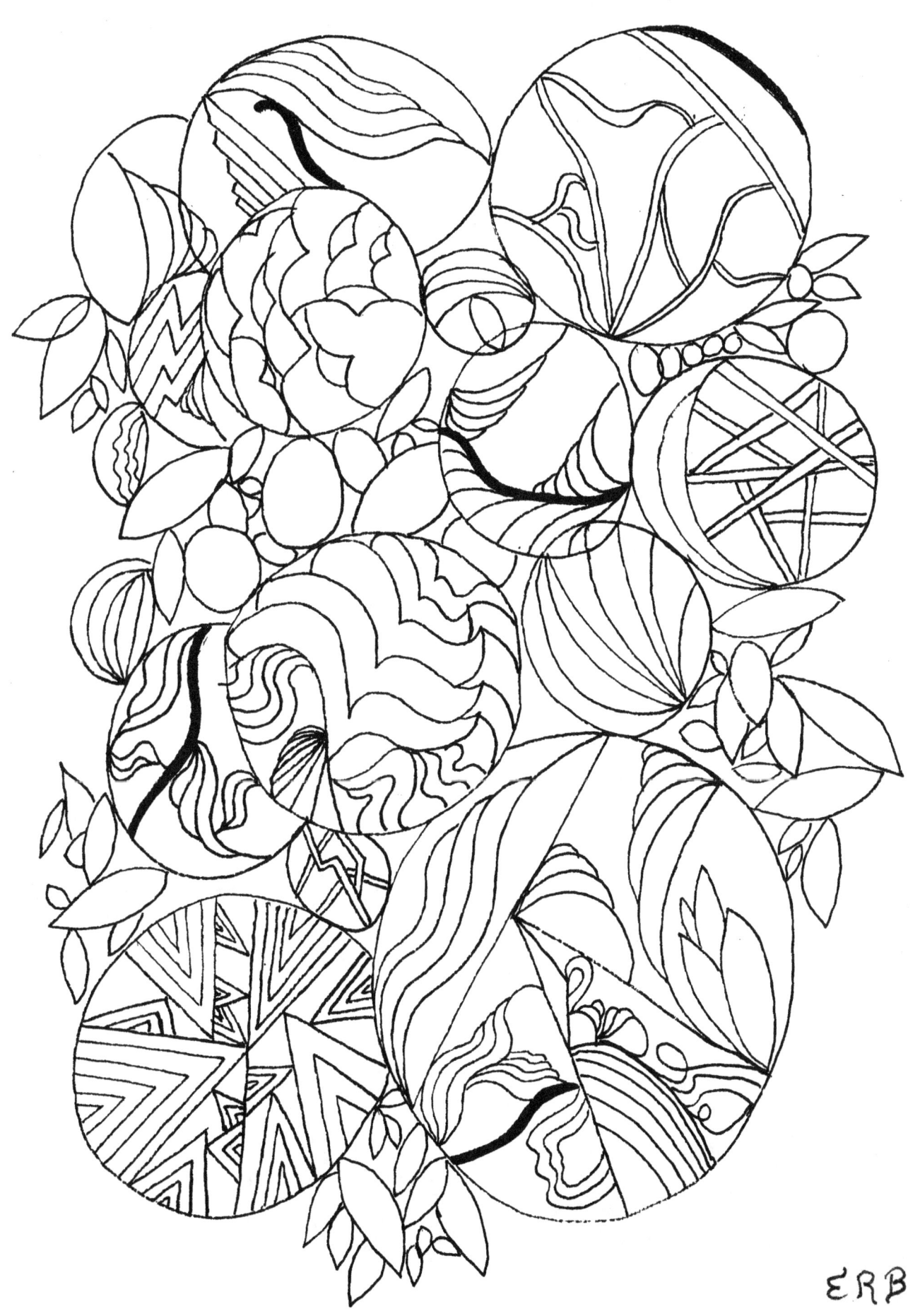

ERB

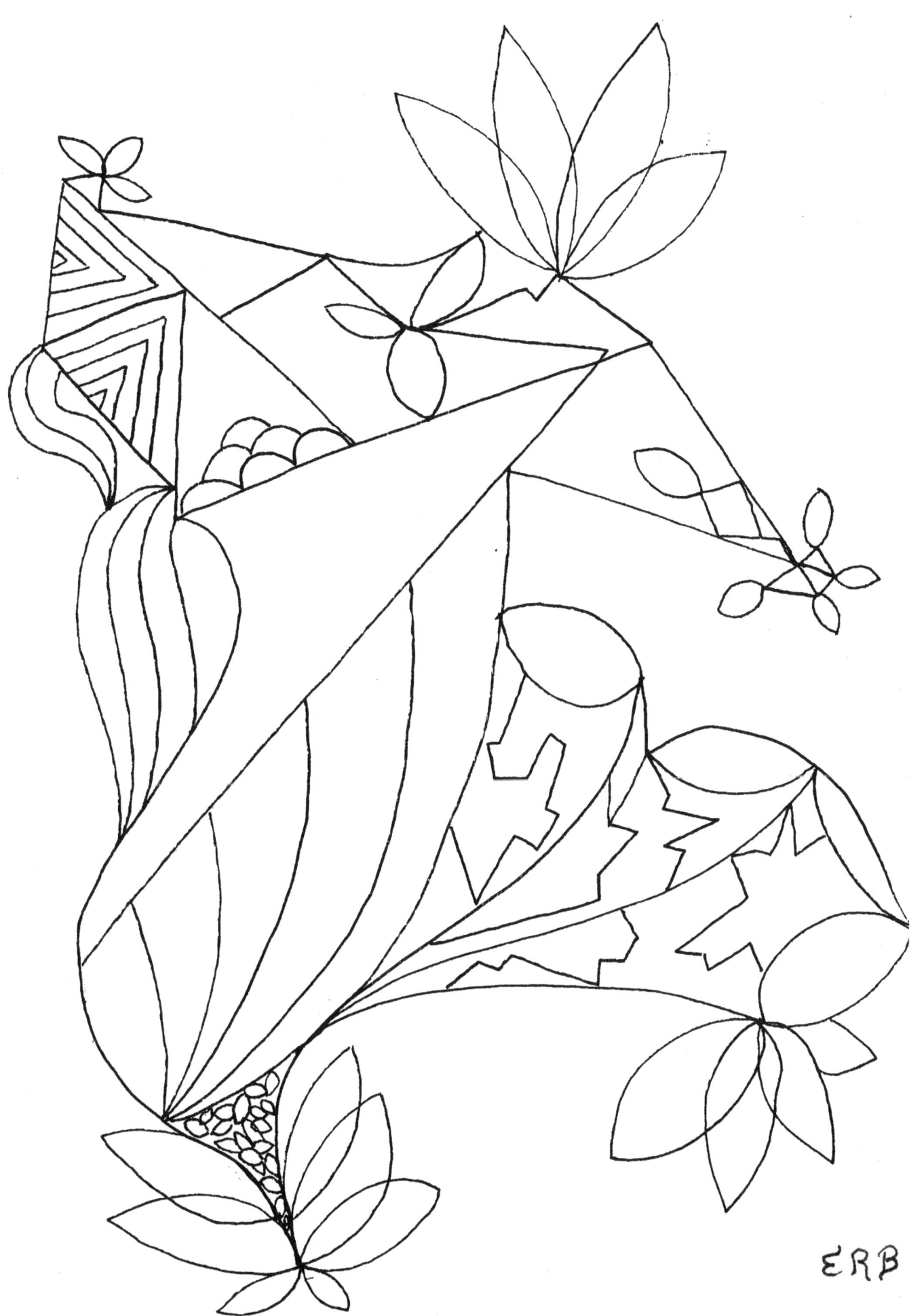

ERB

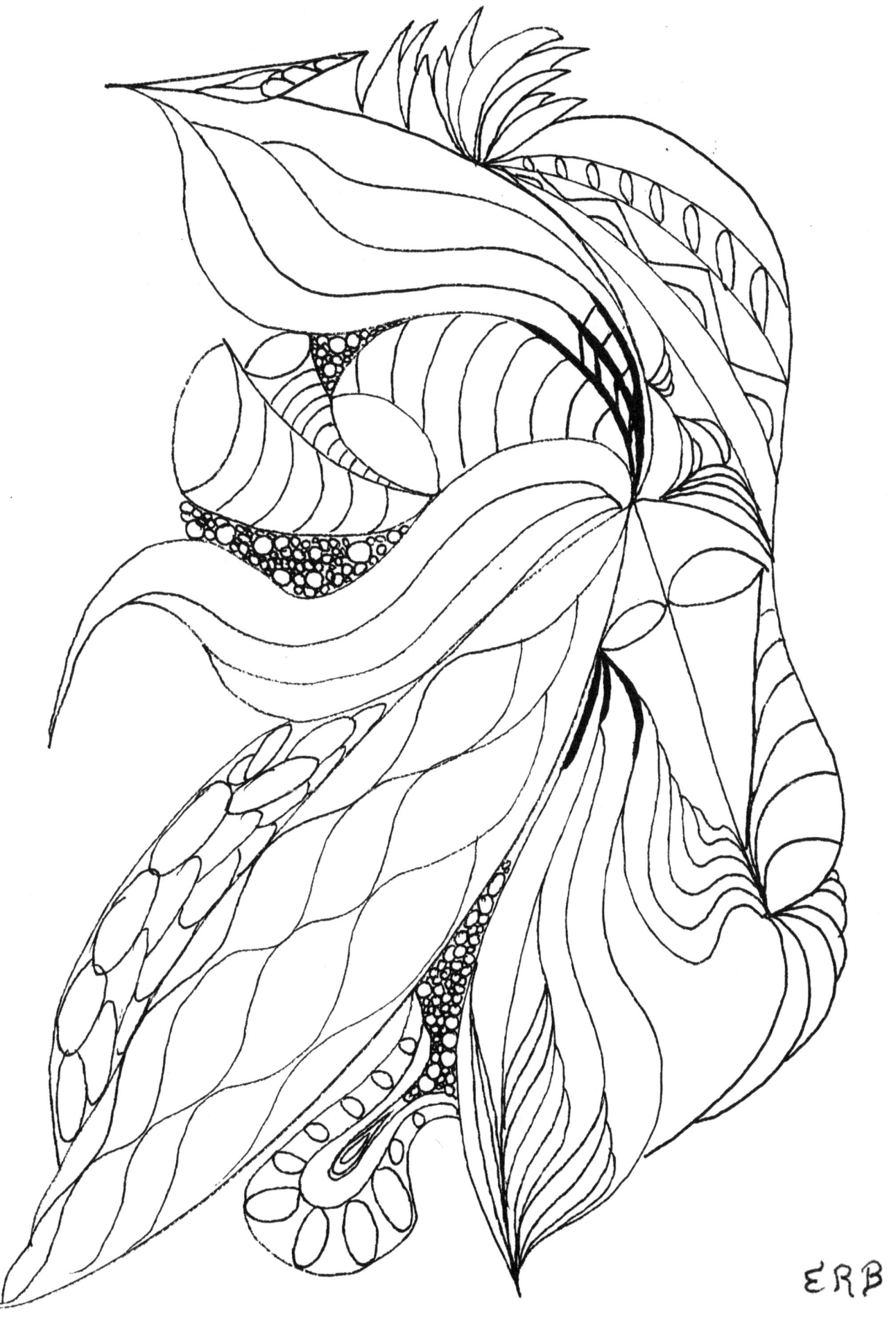

ERB

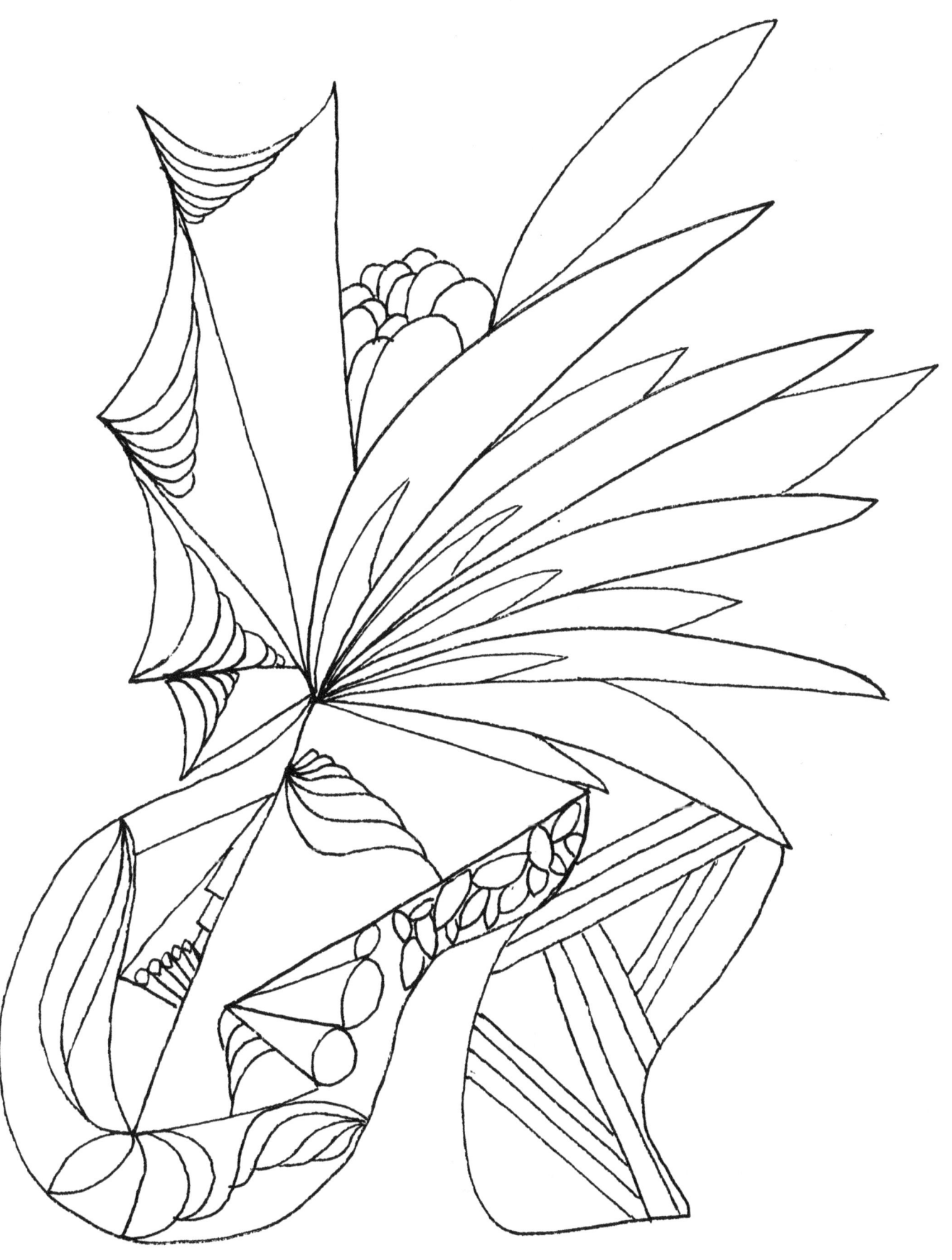

ERB

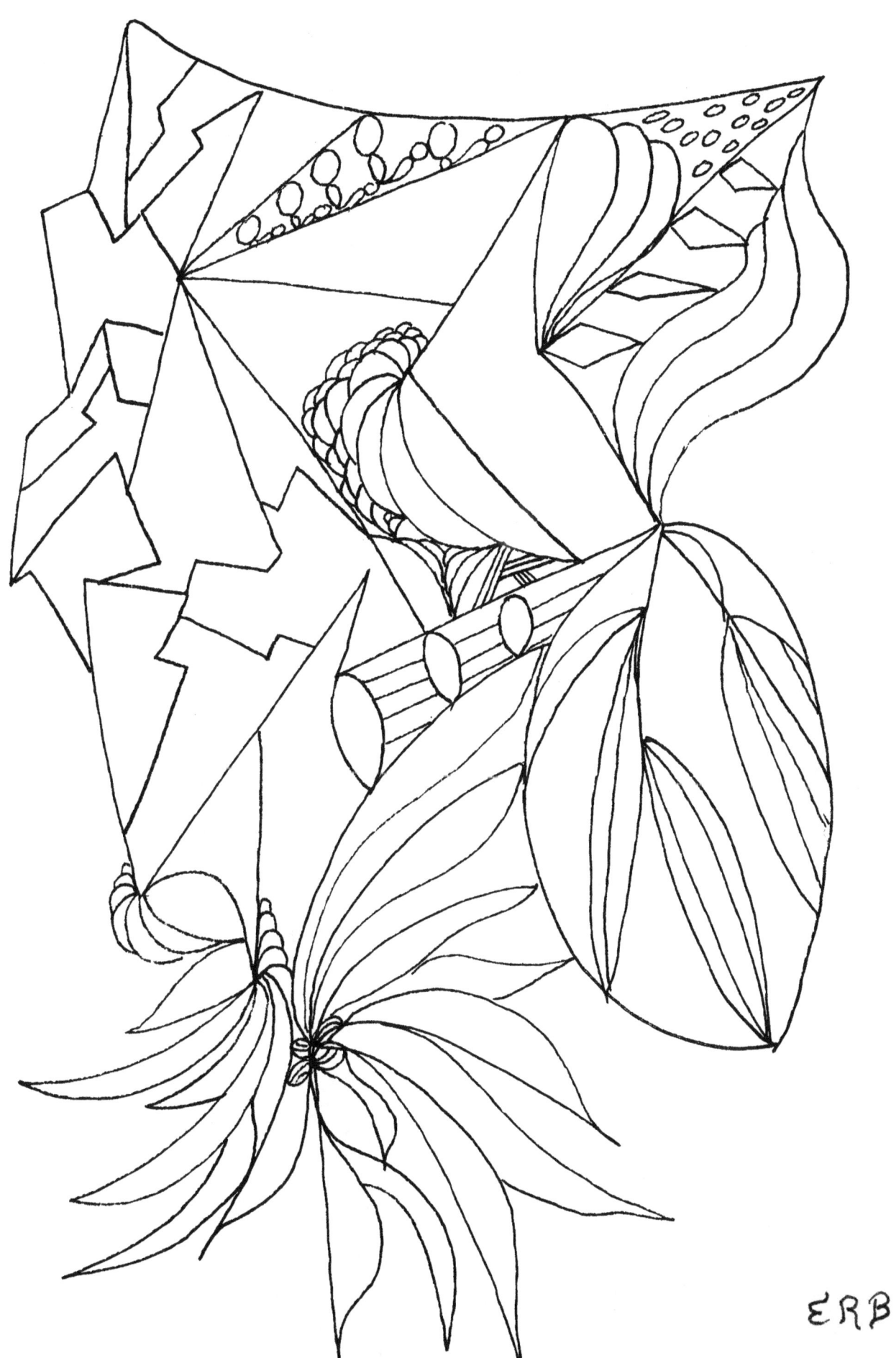

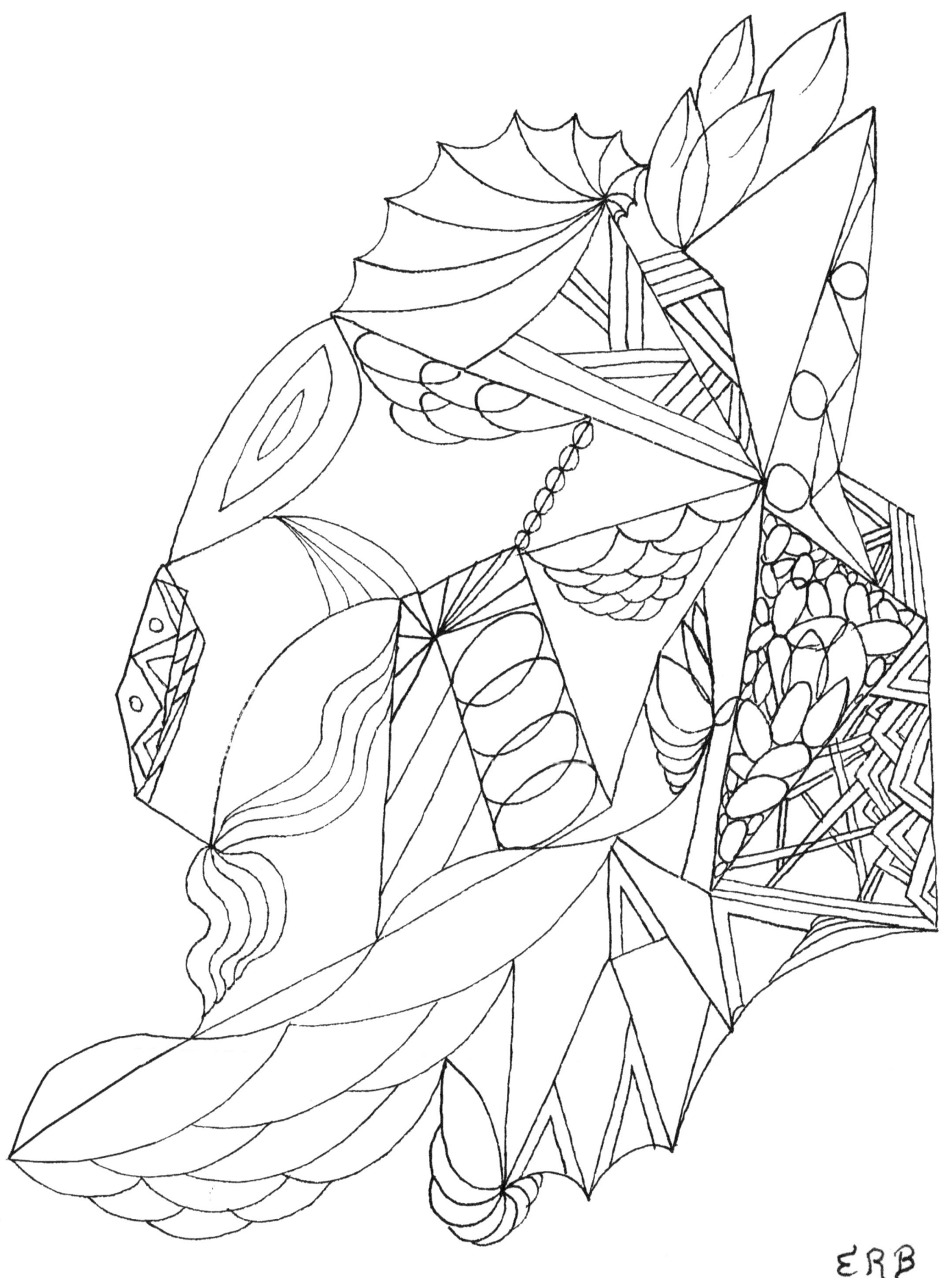

ERB

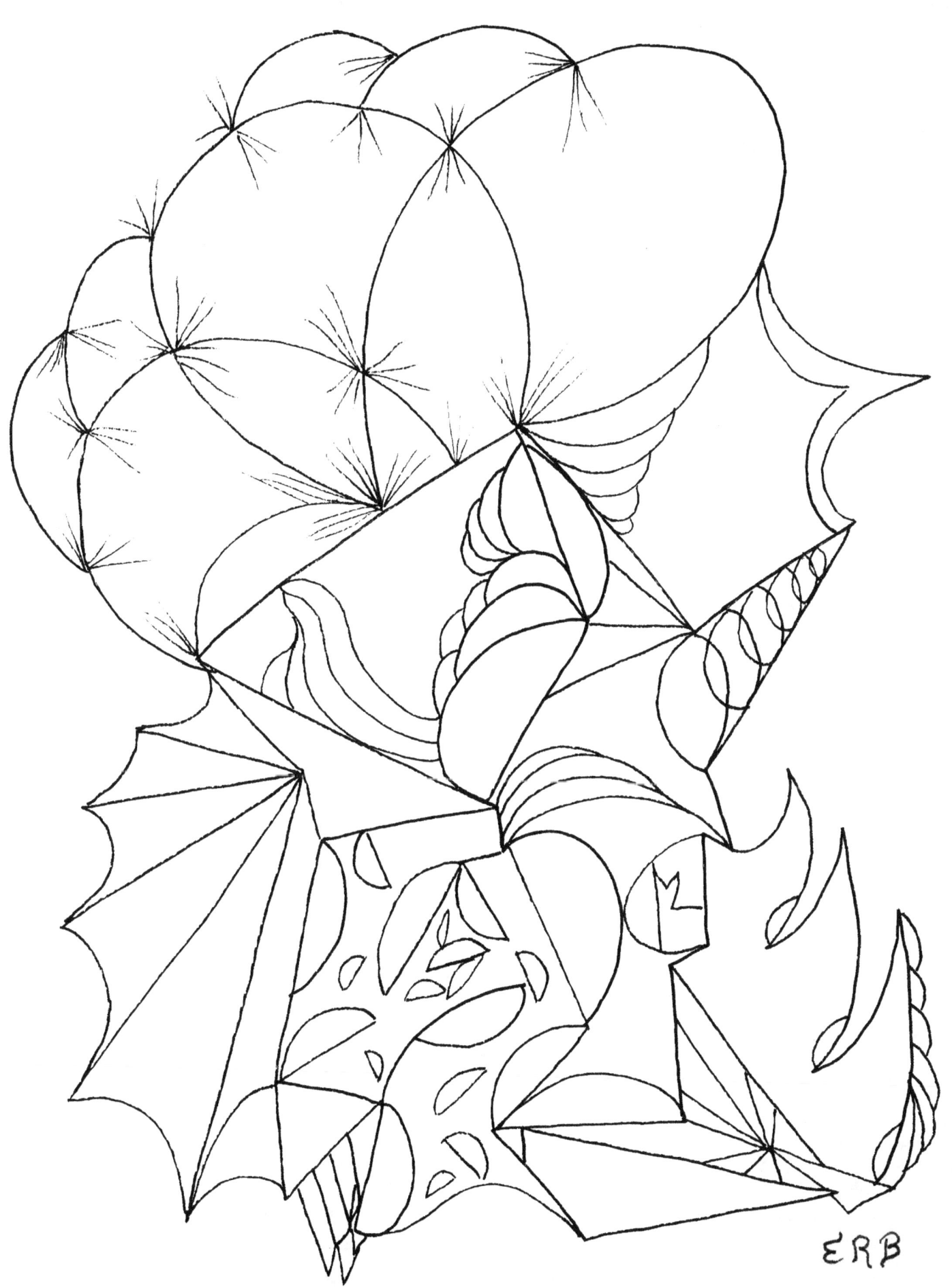

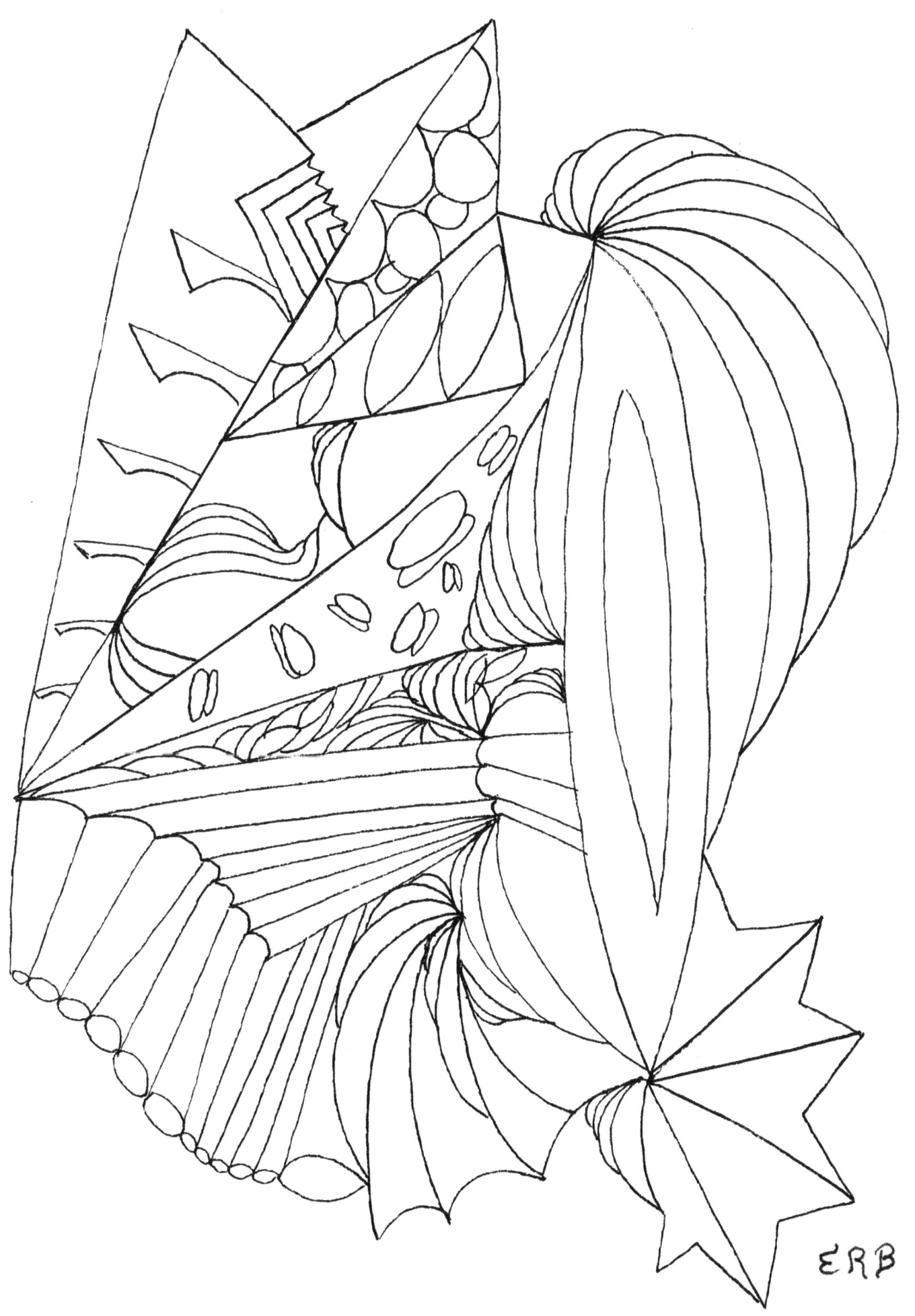

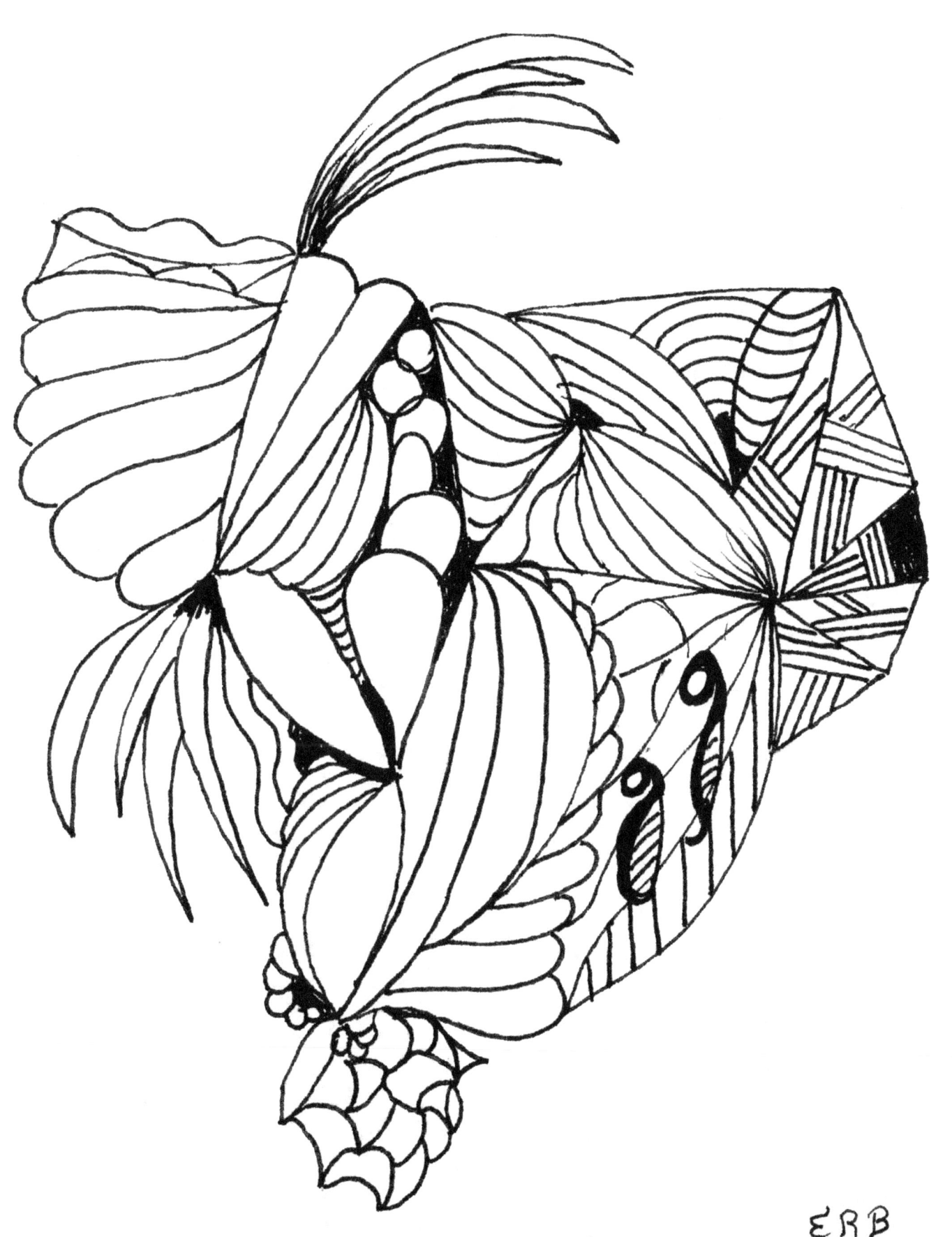

ERB

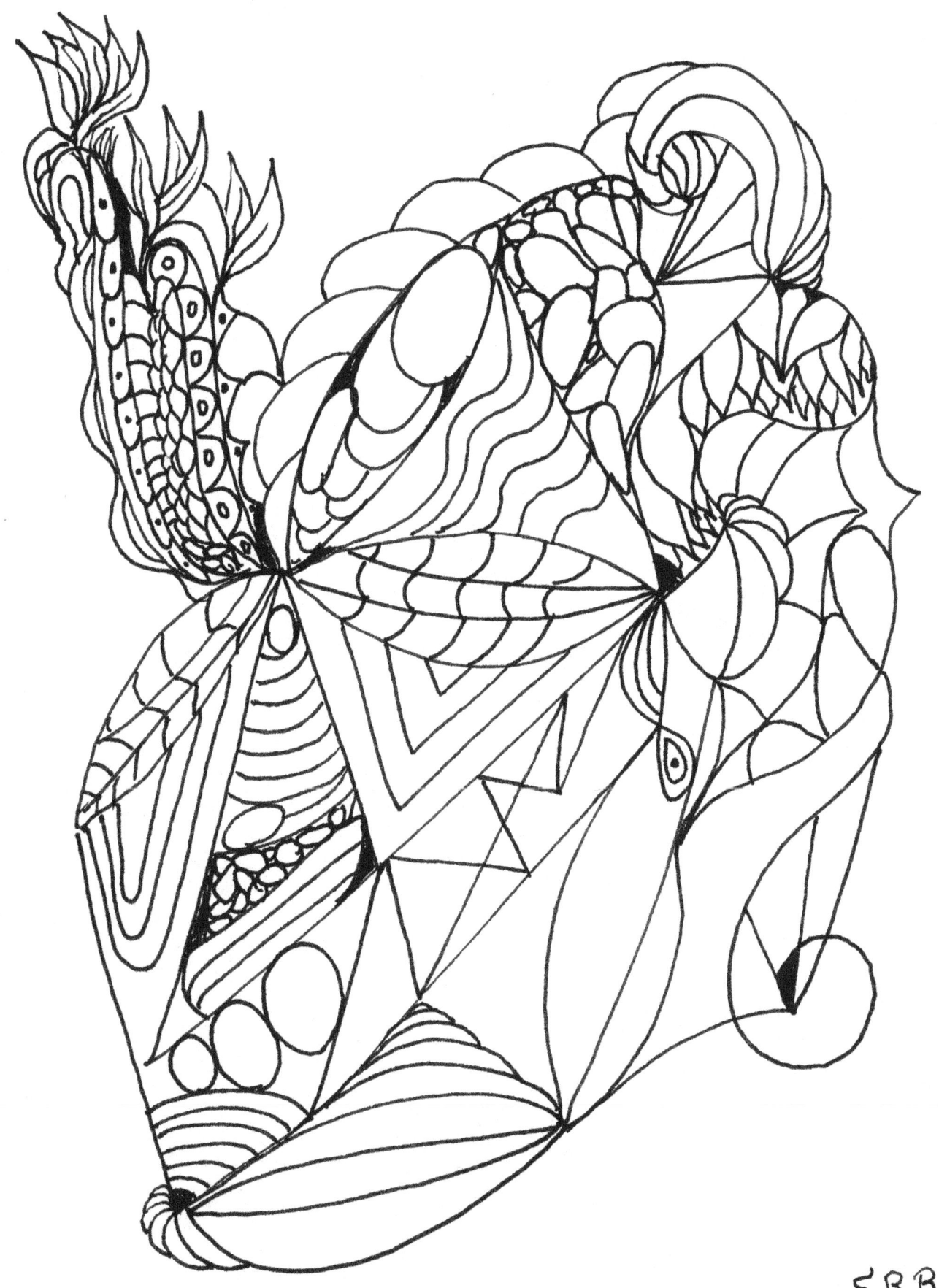

ERB

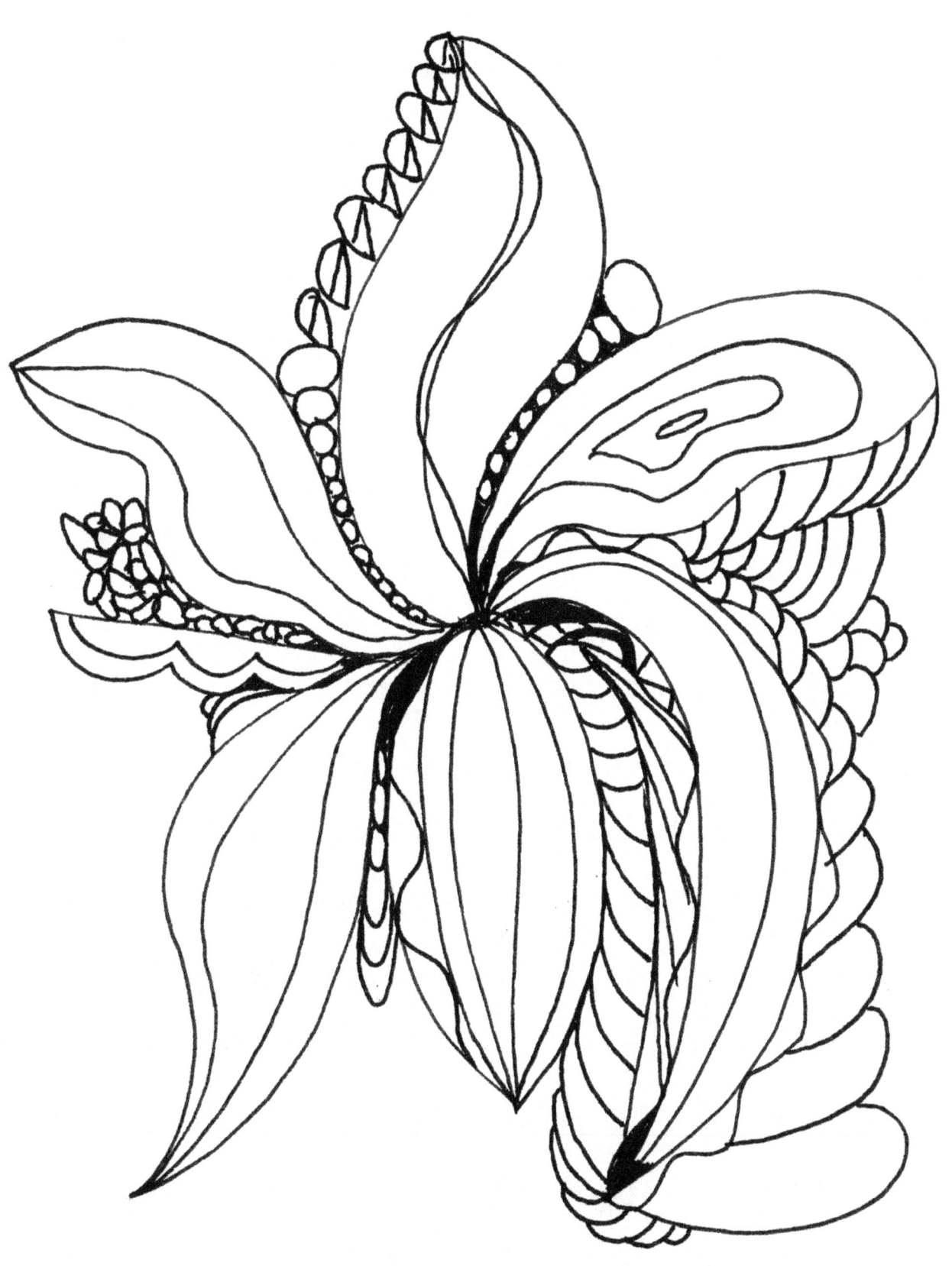

ERB

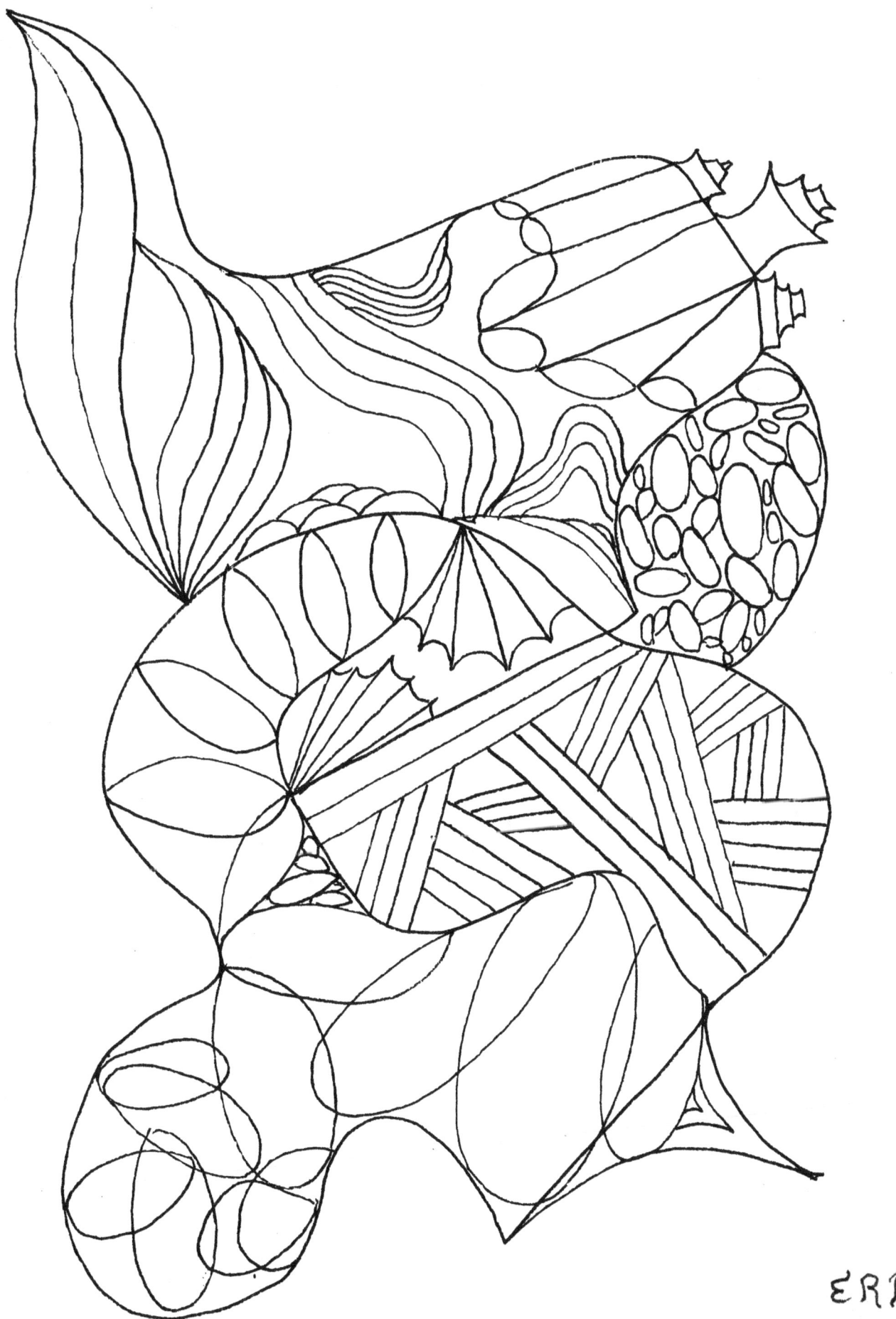

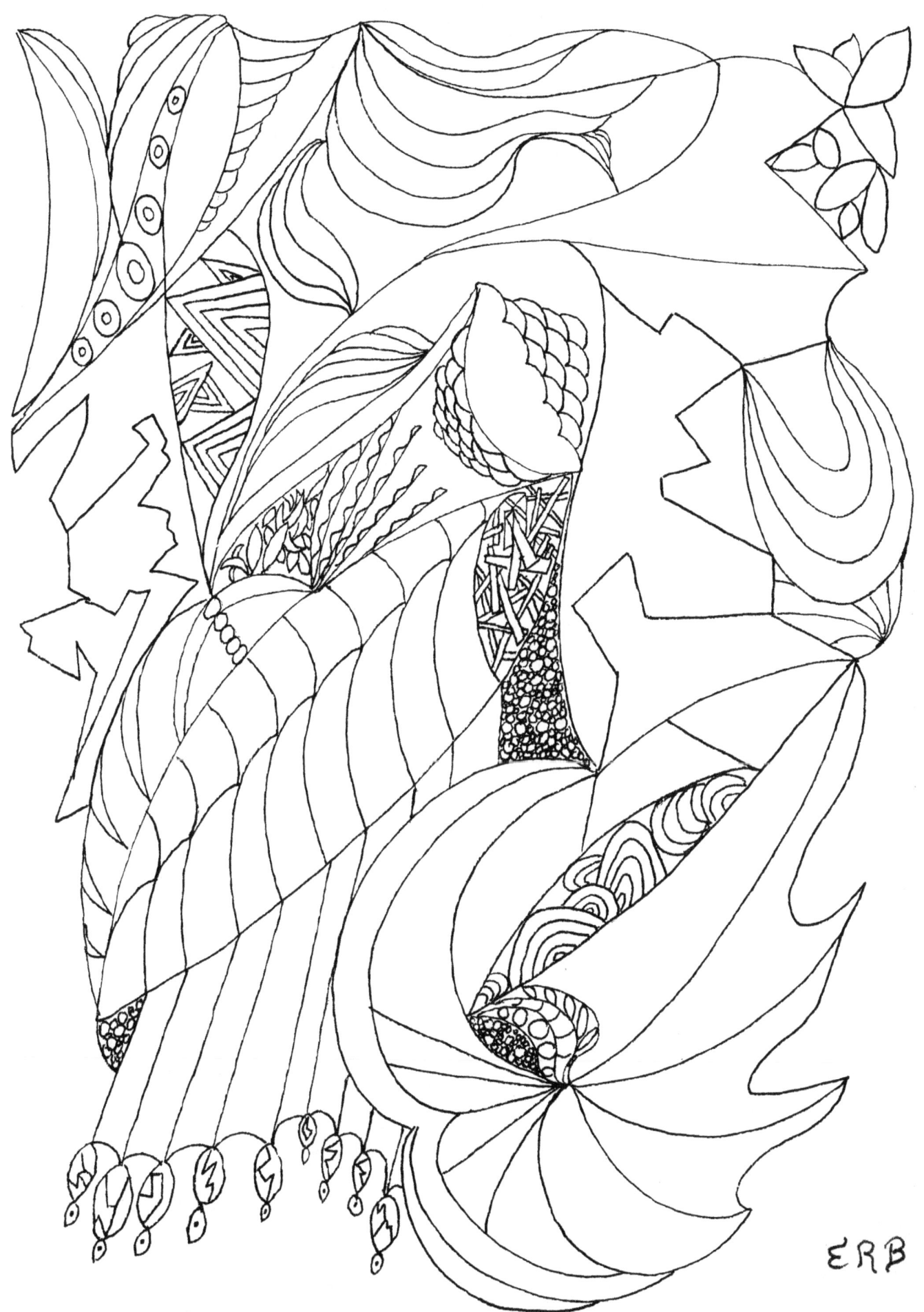

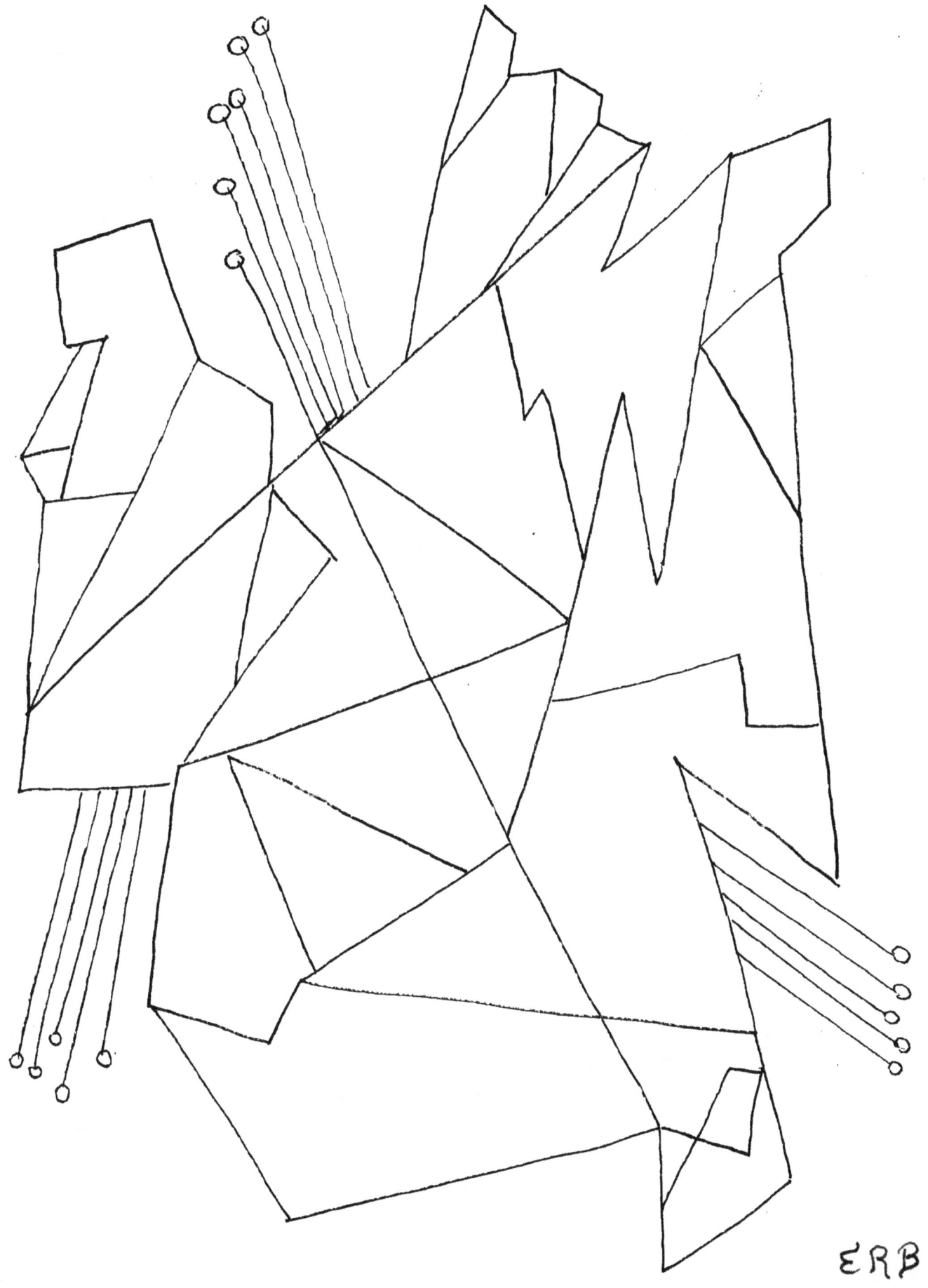

ERB

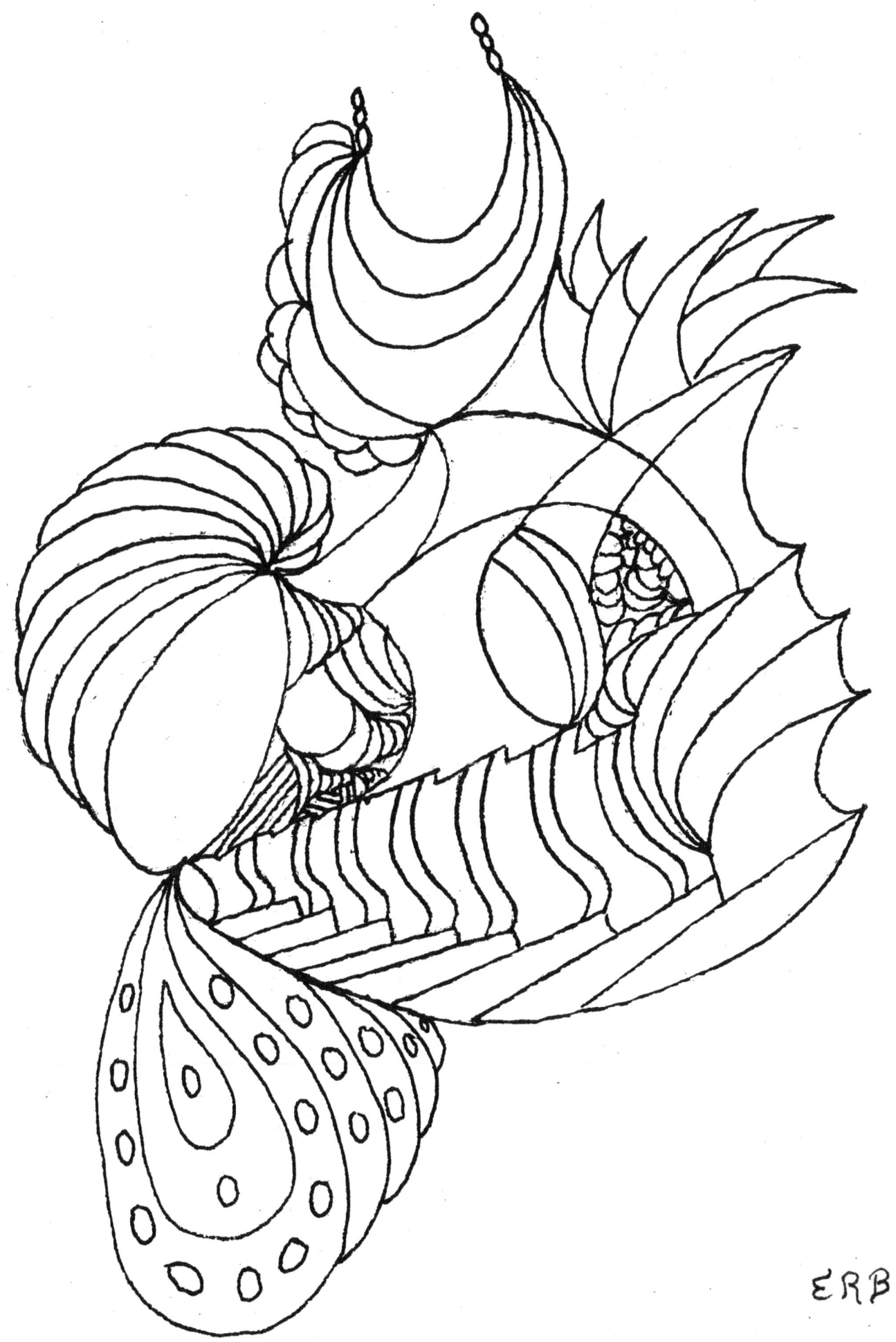

ERB

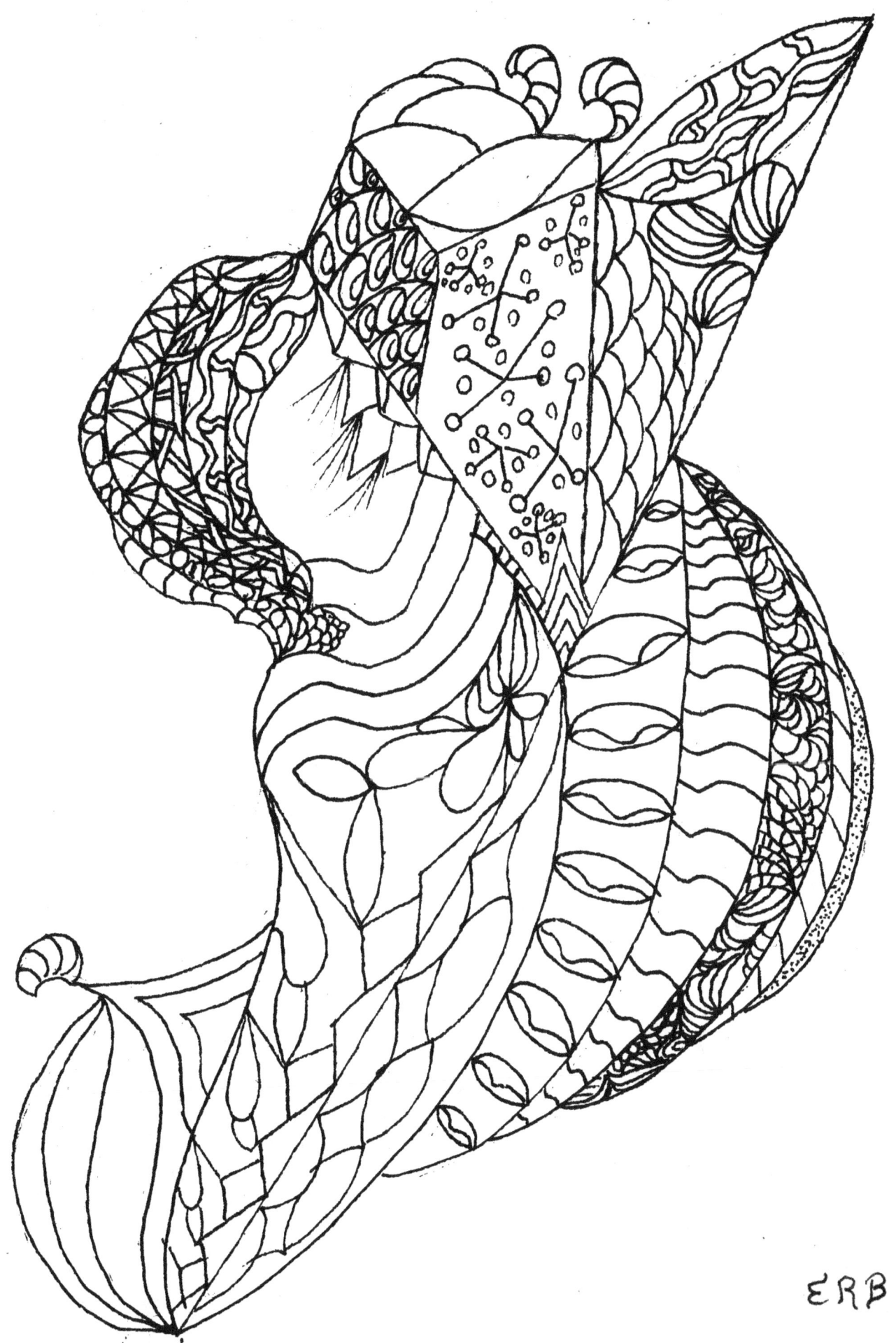

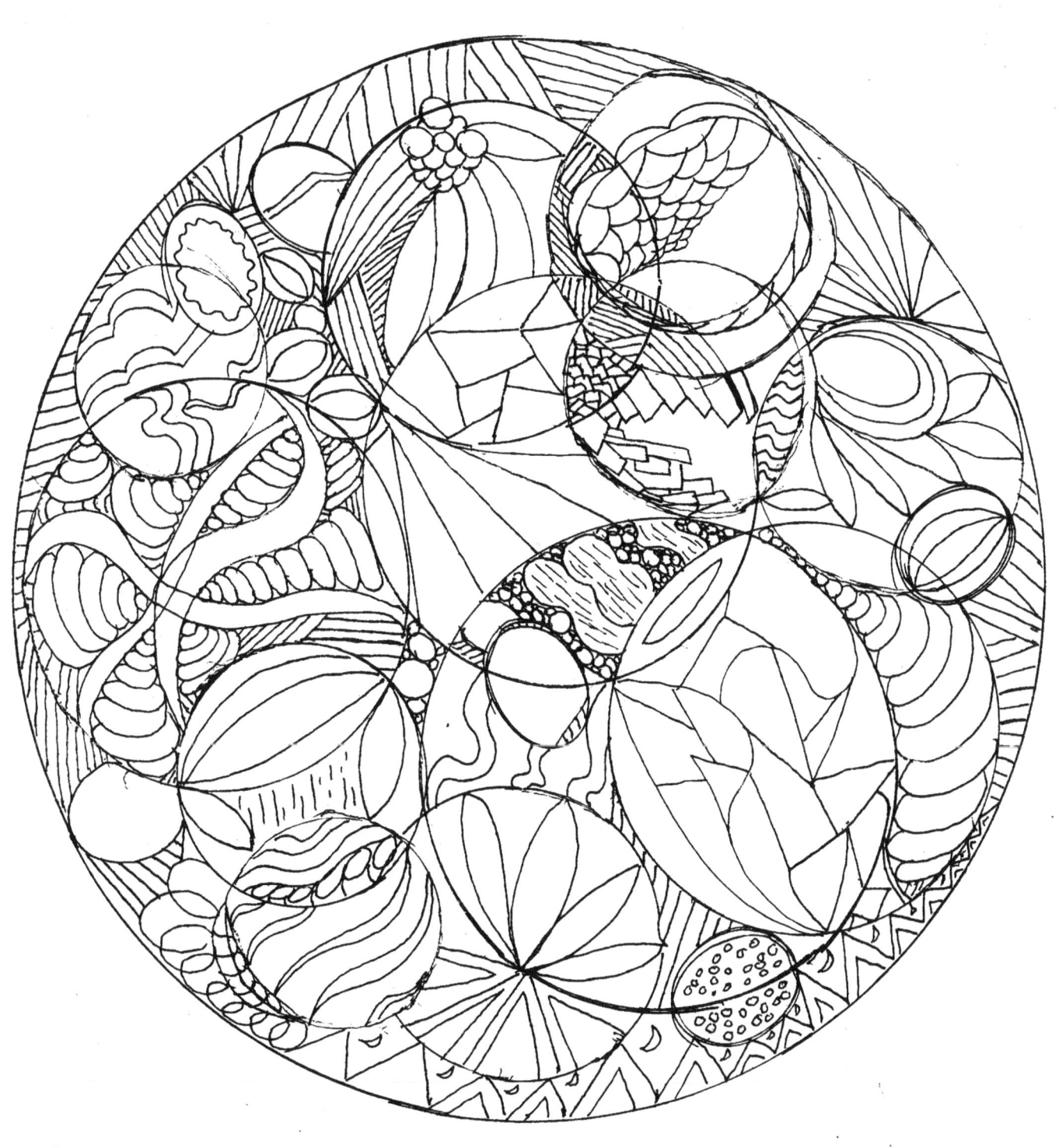

ERB

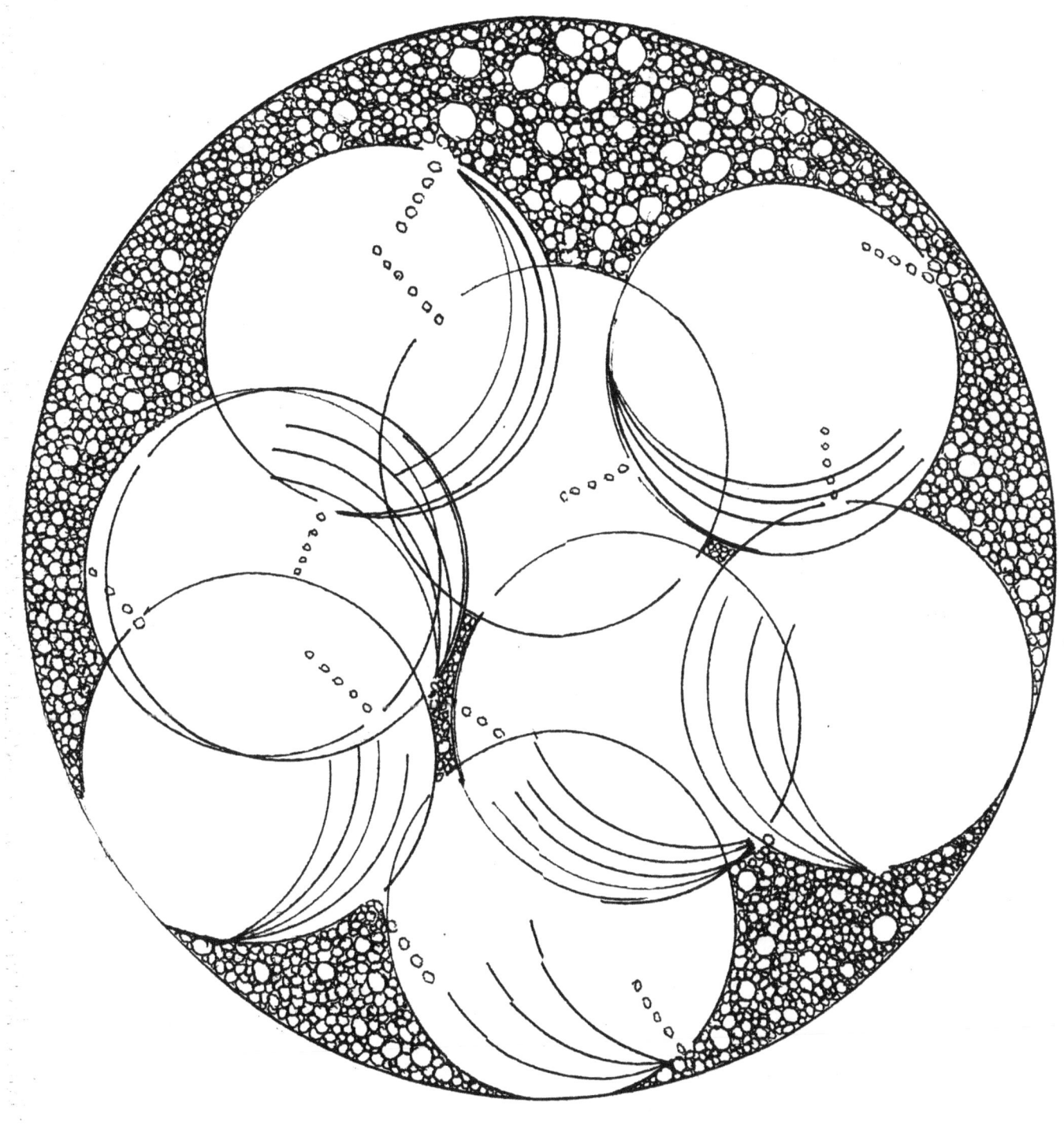

ERB